# The warnings of the New Testament

The message of many frequently avoided New
Testament passages

Anastasios Kioulachoglou

Also by the same author:


Tithing, giving and the New Testament

and many teaching articles in the Journal of Biblical Accuracy

**Visit our website for free downloads, ordering and subscriptions.**


# www.jba.gr

# DEDICATION

To my wife for her love and to the brother who read this first and helped me with his comments.

# TABLE OF CONTENTS

# INTRODUCTION

In Acts 20:26-27 we find Paul speaking to the Ephesian elders. Making a summary of his ministry, he told them:

"Therefore I testify to you this day that I am innocent of the blood of all, for *I did not shrink from declaring to you the whole counsel of God.*"

Paul did not shrink, did not withhold from telling the Ephesians, and the church of God in general, *the whole counsel of God*. One could say that one more study on the matter of salvation would really be redundant, as salvation is something very fundamental and one would expect that we would all get it right. But I do not think we do. At least this is my own experience. I was born a Greek Orthodox, went as a kid to catechism and followed the liturgies etc. However, I was already a teenager and had never heard about salvation by grace through faith. My conclusion at that time was that God is a rather harsh figure waiting for me to do something wrong so that He can punish me. Of course this is not true and I found it out a few years later, at the age of 21, when I met the true, living and loving God. Then for the first time I heard about the Bible being the Word of God and about salvation by grace through faith. This was so liberating! God was not a distant figure any more. He was a real God, as real as I saw Him in the Bible.

The main teaching I received was that once a man believes he is immediately, once and for all, saved, regardless of what he will do with his faith in his life. However, in the more than two decades since then, I had various trials and temptations which made me realize that staying in the faith is not something automatic, something that can be considered as given right from the moment that somebody believed. What I understood is that faith is a rather continuous than a one-off decision.

In these 25 years I have seen friends who were so happy in the beginning when I told them about Christ and were all for it, praising God, praying etc., only to get mad at me and God soon after, not wanting to hear anything about Him any more. Why? Because a girlfriend abandoned them or because a relative told them that all this was "heretic" etc. In time of temptation and tribulation because of God's Word they did not hold up. I have also seen others who though they accepted Christ, were eventually carried away by their simultaneous love for the world, which choked, the seed of the Word exactly as the parable of the sower says. Thus Christ became to them someone they once heard about but the fruit or the difference He made to them nobody could really see. In addition, I came across many warnings and initially puzzling scriptures that did not appear to reconcile with the doctrine according to which a person who once is saved is always saved regardless of whether they later, for various reasons, essentially discontinue in the faith.

The present study looks at a multitude of Scriptures from the New Testament, that make clear that faith is more a race that has to be run to the end than a one-off event which upon happening it is guaranteed that will be valid forever. Staying in the faith, ending the race, is neither automatic nor it is guaranteed for all those who start the race. Some, as the examples I gave above, in the first difficulties and trials drop out. Others have a very strong love for the things of the world and they too move away. Only some of those who start the race really run it to the end. This, as we will see, is very clear from the New Testament.

## WARNING! NARROW GATE, DIFFICULT PATH AHEAD!

Not many like narrow and difficult roads, but it is clear from what the Lord tells us that the road of faith is just that: a difficult way passing through a narrow gate:

Matthew 7:13-14
"Enter by the narrow gate; for wide is the gate and broad is the way that leads to destruction, and there are many who go in by it. *Because narrow is the gate and difficult is the way which leads to life,* and there are few who find it."

Warnings along a difficult, narrow road are very important, for we can easily move away. And moving away in our case means to a road that is easy and wide i.e. to a road that feels good to the five senses. Who has driven on a narrow path and has not paid full attention to the warnings? Who has thought while on such a path that the warnings are there to terrify him (instead of keeping him on the road) or that perhaps they are not relevant to him but refer to some other drivers? I think none of us does this. Equally speaking, there are many warnings in the New Testament and their purpose is to alert us, so that we keep on the right path, especially since the right path is also a narrow, difficult path. As we would never ignore the warnings on any difficult path, so also we must not ignore or explain away the warnings given in the Word of God concerning the difficult path of faith, for they are there for our good. Our purpose in this study is to bring out these warnings.

## FOR WHOM IS THIS BOOK WRITTEN?

This book does not speak – with the exception of the first chapter - about the great realities of being born again, the great realities of having the spirit of God in you, the great realities of being a child of God by faith etc. Many of us have heard about these realities already. The problem however is that some have heard about them in a rather unbalanced way, without hearing also or taking seriously into consideration all passages on the matter and especially those dealt with in this study. Thus they have concluded that these truths and salvation in particular are based on a first moment of faith, after which we are forever saved, regardless of what happens to our faith after that moment. This is the main audience of this book, and our main purpose here is to balance out, through focusing exclusively to the warnings of the New Testament, some of the imbalances created because of the almost complete ignorance of these warnings.

# 1

## SALVATION: WHAT DOES IT TAKE?

Faith in the resurrected Jesus Christ as Lord, the Christ, the Messiah, the Son of God is undeniably the only way for somebody to get saved. This is very clear from a multitude of Scriptures. Here are some:

John 3:14-18
"And as Moses lifted up the serpent in the wilderness, so must the Son of Man be lifted up, that whoever believes in him may have eternal life. "For God so loved the world, that he gave his only Son, that *whoever believes in him should not perish but have eternal life.* For God did not send his Son into the world to condemn the world, but in order that the world might be saved through him. Whoever believes in him is not condemned, but whoever does not believe is condemned already, because he has not believed in the name of the only Son of God."

John 20:30-31
"Now Jesus did many other signs in the presence of the disciples, which are not written in this book; but these are written *so that you may believe that Jesus is the Christ, the Son of God, and that by believing you may have life in his name.*"

John 11:25-26
"I am the resurrection and the life. *Whoever believes in me*, though he dies, yet shall he live, and everyone who lives and believes in me shall never die."

Mark 16:15-16
"And he said to them, "Go into all the world and proclaim the gospel to the whole creation. *Whoever believes and is baptized will be saved*, but whoever does not believe will be condemned."

Acts 16:30-31
"And brought them [Paul and Silas] out, and said, Sirs, what must I do to be saved? And they [Paul and Silas] said, *Believe on the Lord Jesus Christ*, and you will be saved, you and your household."

Romans 10:9
"if you confess with your mouth that Jesus is Lord, and *believe* in your heart that God raised him from the dead, you will be saved."

Before saying anything else, I would first like to point out that in the "whoever believes" and the other similar statements given in the above passages, the *present tense* is used. In other words, what is described here is an active, present faith and not a past event that perhaps may or may not hold true now. An even more accurate translation of these statements would be "whoever goes on believing" i.e. believes now and goes on believing. This would correspond more to the fact that the present tense in ancient Greek was used to point out *duration* rather than one-off events. The first appendix of this book gives more insight to this and the usage of the present tense in ancient Greek.

Back to our subject: it is obvious from the passages we gave above (and there are more) that we are not saved through works of the law or our own works. Salvation is given free, by grace, as a gift to everyone who *believes* in Jesus Christ as his Lord, the Messiah, the Son of God. This is the undisputed truth of

God's Word. Faith therefore is the one key to salvation with grace being the other key. Ephesians 2:8 summarizes this very well:

Ephesians 2:8
"For *by grace you have been saved through faith*; and this is not of yourselves: it is the gift of God"

There are two components that when combined give salvation: grace and faith. Each of them alone cannot give salvation. The grace of God alone cannot save a person if this person does not have faith i.e. if he does not honestly and truly believe, from the heart, in Jesus Christ as his Lord, as the Son of God and Messiah.

Basically God wants *everybody* to be saved and gave His Son for *everybody* as a ransom. As 1 Timothy 2:3-6 says:

"This is good, and it is pleasing in the sight of God our Savior, *who desires all people to be saved* and to come to the knowledge of the truth. "For there is one God, and one mediator between God and men, the man Christ Jesus; Who *gave himself a ransom for all*, to be testified in due time."

And also Titus 2:11
"For *the grace of God that brings salvation has appeared to all men*"

Jesus Christ gave Himself for everybody! God wants everybody to be saved. His grace has appeared to *all* men. Therefore, the grace of God  - the first part of the salvation condition of Ephesians 2:8 ("by *grace*") - is available to everybody; it "has appeared to all men". But the second part ("through *faith*") is not there in everybody. Only some truly believe in what God says in His Word about His Son and only these will be saved, for salvation is not just by grace, but "by grace *through faith*".

Having clarified this point, the critical question is: once somebody believes, is faith something guaranteed to last forever or is it something that has to be kept, which in turn means that it can also be abandoned? How does the Bible treat faith? Does it treat it as something dynamic or as something static i.e. as something that once you have it, you will always have it? What does it mean to have true faith? What happens to salvation, in case the faith is abandoned? Is this possible at all and if yes what are the consequences? Many people do not bother to ask these questions. In this study we will ask these questions, and see the plain answers the Bible gives, starting from the most appropriate person to speak about salvation: the Savior Himself and then continuing with the teachings of His apostles, given in the epistles.

# 2

## THE PARABLE OF THE SOWER

To start let's go to the well-known parable of the sower, mentioned in three out of the four gospels. We will read here the record of Luke:

Luke 8:5-8, 11-15
"A sower went out to sow his seed. And as he sowed, some fell along the path and was trampled underfoot, and the birds of the air devoured it. And some fell on the rock, and as it grew up, it withered away, because it had no moisture. And some fell among thorns, and the thorns grew up with it and choked it. And some fell into good soil and grew and yielded a hundredfold." As he said these things, he called out, "He who has ears to hear, let him hear. .... Now the parable is this: The seed is the word of God. The ones along the path are those who have heard; then the devil comes and takes away the word from their hearts, so that they may not believe and be saved. And the ones on the rock are those who, when they hear the word, receive it with joy. But these have no root; they believe for a while, and in time of testing fall away. And as for what fell among the thorns, they are those who hear, but as they go on their way they are choked by the cares and riches and pleasures of life, and their fruit does not mature. As for

that in the good soil, they are those who, hearing the word, hold it fast in an honest and good heart, and bear fruit with patience."

We have in this parable all the possible outcomes of the seed of the Word of God. As we see, in the first category the Word did not enter in the hearts of the recipients. They did not believe it. In contrast, the second and third categories received the Word but none of the two brought forth fruit. Why, we will see in the next section. Finally, the fourth category was the only one that heard the Word, received it and bore fruit. Our focus in this chapter will be on the second and third categories of this parable, as these relate more to the topic of this study.

## 2.1. "THOSE WHO FELL ON THE ROCK"

For the second category we read:

"And the ones on the rock are those who, when they hear the word, receive it with joy. But these have no root; *they believe for a while*, and in time of testing fall away."

Did the people in this category believe? The answer of the Lord is yes they did. They *"believe for a while"*, He said. So we immediately see that faith has a *time* dimension. In other words, the fact that somebody believes does not necessarily mean that he will believe for the rest of his life. It may be that he believes but only "for a while". Once this "a while" is over then he is no longer in the faith, like it happened to the people of this category here. They started well, but after the start, after "a while", in time of temptation or persecution on account of the Word (Mark 4:7) they fell away. Several examples of this category come to mind: people who heard the Word, accepted it and then shared it with their relatives and friends only to be rejected by them. Instead of holding on accepting the stigma they gave up and departed from the faith. Others had also the same bright beginning. Then a temptation arose (it can be anything) and they gave in, perhaps got offended with God and His people and they also departed. These people had once believed, but they did not believe any more. In fact the word translated as "fall away" is the Greek word "aphistemi", which means "to withdraw from; hence, to fall away, to apostatize" (Vine's dictionary). So, yes, it is possible for people who believed, under tribulation and temptation for the Word, to depart, to apostatize. This is exactly what happened with those in the second category of the parable of the sower. God was once their choice but they departed from Him, abandoning the faith.

Now the critical question is: if these people do not return and repent, will they be saved? If we are to believe the doctrine according to which it is enough that somebody believes even for a while and he will be saved, regardless of what will happen to his faith afterwards, then yes these will be saved for they had believed. However, the problem with this view is that it ignores the fact that faith is not something static, something that, because one had it sometime, somewhere, is also guaranteed that he will never abandon it. On the contrary, faith has a time dimension. And when people give up the faith, believing only *for a while*, they also leave back what was promised to them due to their faith, namely salvation, eternal life. Because really salvation is not just through grace, but "by grace through faith". Grace is God's part and faith is our part. Both conditions have to be held and God always keeps His. But whoever departs from the faith leaves also whatever he got through faith, i.e. the promise of salvation. The New Testament has plenty of passages that make this very clear and the purpose of this book is to bring them out.

To find a way to explain the above passage some support that the people of the second category of the parable of the sower were never true believers, for had they been true believers - they say - they would have never fallen away. But obviously this view contradicts what the Lord Himself said when He explained this part of the parable. According to Him: "And the ones on the rock are those who, when they hear the word, *receive it with joy*. But these have no root; *they believe for a while*, and in time of testing *fall away"*. These people received the Word just like you and me: with joy. And they believed it. The Lord did not say that they pretended to believe it, nor did He say that they pretended to have accepted it with joy. In contrast their faith was originally genuine and real. However, it did not last. It endured, but only for a while.  Therefore, it is the duration of the faith that was the problem with these people and not whether the faith existed at all in the beginning, for as we read they really believed, *but* only "for a while".

Perhaps this can explain the agony of Paul to learn about the status of the faith of the persecuted Thessalonians (2 Thessalonians 1:4). As he said to them:

1 Thessalonians 3:1-8
"Therefore *when we could bear it no longer,* we were willing to be left behind at Athens alone, and we sent Timothy, our brother and God's coworker in the gospel of Christ, to establish and exhort you in your faith that no one be moved by these afflictions. For you yourselves know that we are destined for this. For when we were with you, we kept telling you beforehand that we were to suffer affliction, just as it has come to pass, and just as you know. *For this reason, when I could bear it no longer, I sent to learn about your faith, for fear that somehow the tempter had tempted you and our labor would be in vain.* But now that Timothy has come to us from you, and has brought us *the good news of your faith* and love and reported that you always remember us kindly and long to see us, as we long to see you — for this reason, brothers, in all our distress and affliction we have been comforted about you through your faith. For now we live, *if you are standing fast in the Lord."*

Two times in just a few lines Paul speaks about his agony. He knew that the believers were under persecution and he was eager to learn about the status of their faith. Were they standing fast in the Lord or not? What were the news concerning their faith? Bad or good? This was the question and Paul was urgently waiting to hear its answer from Timothy. Therefore faith is not something unmovable; something that, once you have it, is guaranteed that you will keep forever. If it was like this, Paul would not worry. In that case, since they were once in the faith, they would always be in the faith despite the persecutions and temptations. But it is not like this. The purpose of the tempter, the devil, is to overthrow our faith, to make us take offense with God and His people and depart from the faith. In short, his purpose is to devour us (1 Peter 5:8). The fact that we were standing fast before the tribulation does not mean that we will necessarily also do so after the tribulation or the temptation. We have to make up our mind. God will support us and hold us but we have to hold on too; we have to decide that we will stay with Him, no matter what. Some do this but some do not. Those who do not, abandon the faith. They may not say it publicly, but in reality they do not mind much anymore. I believe that whoever is in the faith for some time knows perhaps some related examples. But let's now pass to the third category of the parable of the sower.

## 2.2. "AND SOME FELL AMONG THORNS"

Moving now to the people in the third category of the parable of the sower: these are the ones who heard the Word, "but as they go on their way they are choked by the cares and riches and pleasures of life, and their fruit does not mature[1]". It is not that these people did not receive the Word. Those who did not receive the Word, because they did not understand it and Satan stole it, were in the first category. In contrast, those in the third category had a heart for the Word, but they had - or they acquired on the way - also a heart for the world, namely the pleasures and cares of this world and the deceitfulness of riches. These acted as thorns chocking the Word with the result that it did not really bear fruit. Thus we see that it is not enough to have the Word in

---

[1] To avoid misunderstanding the phrase "their fruit does not mature" does not mean that they were somehow fruitful. This is obvious by Matthew 13:22 which has this as "and they prove *unfruitful*".

order to bear fruit. The Word on its own does not become fruitful, if the things that act in competition to the Word – the cares of this world (i.e. caring for what the world cares for[2]), the deceitfulness of riches and the pleasures of this life – are not rooted out. If this rooting out does not happen, the result is a worldly, unfruitful "Christian". He may know and originally he may have received the Word but there is no fruit. The other things that were not rooted out made it unfruitful.

Indeed, as the Lord made it very clear, it is impossible to serve two masters. In the long run one of the two will have to go:

Luke 16:13
"*No servant can serve two masters,* for either he will hate the one and love the other, or he will be devoted to the one and despise the other. You cannot serve God and money."

And as He again, in Luke 21:34, warns us:
"But *watch yourselves* lest *your hearts be weighed down with dissipation and drunkenness and cares of this life,* and that day come upon you suddenly like a trap."

Also John tells us:

1 John 2:15-17
" Do not love the world or the things in the world. *If anyone loves the world, the love of the Father is not in him.* For all that is in the world — *the desires of the flesh and the desires of the eyes and pride of life* — is not from the Father but is from the world. And the world is passing away along with its desires, but whoever does the will of God abides forever."

---

[2] We need to make a clarification here: going to work to provide for our family is not a care that will take us away from God. It is in fact an obligation. However being a workaholic is a care that will take us away from God. Basically "cares of this world", means to care about what the world cares, making the interests of the world our interests and way of life.

And James, calling adulterers and adulteresses those who run after the world, says:

James 4:4
"Adulterers and adulteresses! Do you not know that friendship with the world is enmity with God? Whoever therefore wants to be a friend of the world makes himself an enemy of God."

An adulterer is one who is married to somebody but runs after or lusts after somebody else. Those that run after the world, after the cares of this world, the riches, the dissipation and the pleasures of this life are also called adulterers. Why? Because they abandoned Christ the bridegroom and run after the world.

Back to the parable of the sower, those of the 3rd category have followed the deception of riches or serve other masters (cares and pleasures of this world etc.) and hence they cannot serve Christ at the same time.

Now the critical question is: will this fruitless category, if it remains so and does not repent, enter the Kingdom? To phrase it differently: does it really matter concerning salvation whether somebody's faith is a fruitful faith, or is it OK and there is no issue if somebody allows the Word of God to be choked, to be effectively killed, by his simultaneous love for the world? Is it OK if somebody who has confessed Jesus as his Lord abandons Him serving other lords? What will happen in this case? We do not need to think about the answer. The Lord Himself has answered this question, over 2000 years ago and we would do well to pay attention to His answer. By the way, His answer clearly also applies to those of the second category of the parable i.e. those that believed "for a while":

John 15:1-8
"I am the true vine, and my Father is the vinedresser. *Every branch in me that does not bear fruit he takes away,* and every branch that does bear fruit he prunes, that it may bear more fruit. Already you are clean because of the word that I have spoken to you.

23

Abide in me, and I in you. *As the branch cannot bear fruit by itself, unless it abides in the vine, neither can you, unless you abide in me.* I am the vine; you are the branches. Whoever abides in me and I in him, he it is that bears much fruit, for apart from me you can do nothing. *If anyone does not abide in me he is thrown away like a branch and withers; and the branches are gathered, thrown into the fire, and burned.* If you abide in me, and my words abide in you, ask whatever you wish, and it will be done for you. *By this my Father is glorified, that you bear much fruit and so prove to be my disciples."*

I believe that the answer of the Lord leaves no space for doubt: the only way to bear fruit is to abide in the vine, in Him. People who do not bear fruit are people who do not abide in the vine and if this does not change they will be gathered like dried branches and at the end, as the Lord said, they will be burned. What does this mean for those in the 3rd (as well as those in the 2nd) category of the parable of the sower? It means that if they do not repent, returning to the vine and thus bearing, by abiding in the vine, the fruit that marks somebody as a true disciple of Christ, they will have the end of the dry branches of the above passage i.e. they will be "gathered, thrown into the fire and be burned". I know I have perhaps offended some readers here, but did I say this? No, I did not. In contrast it is something the Lord said, speaking to the closest of His disciples and on the very night of His arrest. Now, is what He said a surprise? Is what He said something bizarre? No when we understand that a true Christian is not one who once made a confession but later *practically* abandoned it or never in fact practiced what he confessed. In contrast a true Christian is one who tries to live, to practice, with whatever mistakes may come with practicing, his faith. If we have confessed that Jesus is Lord, yet He is not truly our Lord, then it is obvious that our confession was either not an honest confession or it might have been honest in the past but it no longer holds true. Whether what we confessed is true or not is proved by one and only one standard: the fruit we bear, and bearing the desired fruit becomes possible only by abiding in the vine, in Christ. We saw it in the above passage of John 15 where the Lord said: "bear much

24

fruit and so – i.e. by bearing much fruit – prove to be my disciples". Therefore, the fruit we bear is the proof of whether or not we are true disciples of Christ.

In fact, the Lord gave the same measure, the measure of the fruit, to help us discern between false and true prophets:

Matthew 7:15-20
"Beware of false prophets, who come to you in sheep's clothing but inwardly are ravenous wolves. *You will recognize them by their fruits*. Are grapes gathered from thornbushes, or figs from thistles? So, every healthy tree bears good fruit, but the diseased tree bears bad fruit. A healthy tree cannot bear bad fruit, nor can a diseased tree bear good fruit. *Every tree that does not bear good fruit is cut down and thrown into the fire. Thus you will recognize them by their fruits.*"

Many are afraid to speak about fruit, because they think it lessens the grace. It does not! Can an apple tree not produce apples? Trees produce fruit, and the seed of the Word, when it is taken care of, does exactly this: it produces fruit. Faith comes first, then the fruit follows. What is really more unnatural than trees that are supposed to bear fruit and yet remain unfruitful? Would we call such trees healthy? If you had such a tree in your garden and expected fruit from it, as God expects from us, would you say that "it does not matter"? I do not think so.

Fruit is absolutely natural for a Christian and it is absolutely unnatural when it is missing. As Ephesians 2:8-10 makes clear:

Ephesians 2:8-10
"For by grace you have been saved through faith. And this is not your own doing; it is the gift of God, not a result of works, so that no one may boast. For we are his workmanship, *created in Christ Jesus for good works*, which God prepared beforehand, that we should walk in them."

We were not saved by works, yet we were created *for* good works. "Created for" means that this is our destiny, our purpose. To say it differently: cars are "created for" taking us from A to B. Trains are "created for" running on the rail tracks. The apple tree "is created for" producing apples. Equally speaking, *"we are created in Christ Jesus for good works"*. Therefore, good works and faith go hand in hand. It makes really no sense to say that we are in the faith but it does not matter whether we will bring forth the fruit associated with those who are in the faith. It is like saying we are having a car but it does not matter whether it works or not. We all know that it does matter.

That works, being the fruit of a genuine faith, do matter, is made plain by James in his epistle:

James 2:14-17
"What good is it, my brothers, if someone says he has faith but does not have works? Can that faith save him? If a brother or sister is poorly clothed and lacking in daily food, and one of you says to them, "Go in peace, be warmed and filled," without giving them the things needed for the body, what good is that? *So also faith by itself, if it does not have works, is dead."*

"Faith without works is dead", exactly as the body without the spirit is dead. To say it differently, there is no such thing as fruitless, yet true, faith. Fruitless faith is a dead faith and such faith clearly does not get somebody into the Kingdom of God.

Staying a bit more on the crucial subject of works, Paul said several times:

Titus 2:13-14
"waiting for our blessed hope, the appearing of the glory of our great God and Savior Jesus Christ, who gave himself for us to redeem us from all lawlessness and to purify for himself a people for his own possession *who are zealous for good works."*

Titus 3:1
"Remind them to be submissive to rulers and authorities, to be obedient, *to be ready for every good work*"

2 Timothy 2:20-21
"Now in a great house there are not only vessels of gold and silver but also of wood and clay, some for honorable use, some for dishonorable. Therefore, if anyone cleanses himself from what is dishonorable, he will be a vessel for honorable use, set apart as holy, useful to the master of the house, *ready for every good work.*"

And 2 Timothy 3:16-17
"All Scripture is breathed out by God and profitable for teaching, for reproof, for correction, and for training in righteousness, *that the man of God may be complete, equipped for every good work.*"

The Scripture, the Bible, is not there to give us head knowledge. It is not there to make the man of God a theoretical theologian. It is there to make the man of God complete, fruitful, equipped for what he is destined for: *for every good work.*

Going back now to the parable of the sower, only the fourth category bore fruit:

"And some fell into good soil and grew and yielded a hundredfold.... As for that in the good soil, they are those who, hearing the word, *hold it fast in an honest and good heart, and bear fruit with patience.*"

The second and third category of people heard the Word but they did not hold it fast. But this category here, heard the Word and held it fast in a good and honest heart and gave with patience fruit. *Therefore, to bear fruit we need to hold the Word fast in a good and honest heart and with patience we will bear fruit.* This is the key. If, after we receive the Word we allow other things to take it over and move us away from Christ the vine, it will not bear fruit. Guarding our heart with all vigilance (exactly as Proverbs 4:23

tells us), repenting from old practices and renewing the mind to what the Word of God says is therefore very crucial to the outcome of the Word.

Closing this chapter: may we all be in that fourth category and never leave it. Also may those of us who are not in this category return, abiding in the vine and bearing forth the much fruit that brings glory to God and shows whose disciples we truly are. May we check ourselves and if we see thorns may we uproot them and throw them away, instead of essentially deceiving ourselves that we can live with them. We cannot. It is either them or the Lord. One of the two will have to go and we chose which one it will be.

# 3

## A STRAIGHT LOOK AT SOME OF THE "HARD SAYINGS" OF JESUS

It is amazing, but in many western churches we hear so little of what the Lord Himself taught and especially of what many have branded as "hard sayings". However, these sayings are hard only if we try to explain them wearing the glasses of a doctrine that wants salvation to be the result not of a continuing, living faith but of a static, once upon a time faith, that is also allowed to be unfruitful. Then yes, these sayings are very hard to understand. If however we remove these glasses then the sayings of the Lord become *very* clear and obvious.

Before we move further into what the Lord said, I need to say that some have discounted the Lord's sayings under the theory that they do not refer to us, but to Jews living under the law. Thus they classify His sayings to a par little above the Old Testament, and in any case not at all as relevant to us as the epistles, creating like this an artificial antithesis between what the Lord said and what His very disciples said. But as we will see in this study there is no such antithesis. What the Lord said and what His apostles taught are in absolute harmony with each other. Nevertheless and for those familiar with this view, in the second appendix of this study I look at it in more detail, demonstrating why I believe it is false. But let's go on to what the Lord said.

## 3.1. THE PARABLE OF THE UNFAITHFUL SERVANT.

Starting from Matthew 24, the Lord stresses the point of alertness and that we should be awake, waiting for Him to come. Then He further supports His point with three parables, given one after the other, thus showing the great importance He puts on the matter. The first one given is the parable of the unfaithful servant. Let's read it:

Matthew 24:42-51
"Therefore, stay awake, for you do not know on what day your Lord is coming. But know this, that if the master of the house had known in what part of the night the thief was coming, he would have stayed awake and would not have let his house be broken into. Therefore you also must be ready, for the Son of Man is coming at an hour you do not expect. "Who then is the faithful and wise servant, whom his master has set over his household, to give them their food at the proper time? Blessed is that servant whom his master will find so doing when he comes. Truly, I say to you, he will set him over all his possessions. But if that wicked servant says to himself, 'My master is delayed,' and begins to beat his fellow servants and eats and drinks with drunkards, the master of that servant will come on a day when he does not expect him and at an hour he does not know and will cut him in pieces and put him with the hypocrites. In that place there will be weeping and gnashing of teeth."

To whom did Jesus say this parable? Just before He started with it He said to His disciples: "Therefore *you* also must be ready, for the Son of Man is coming at an hour you do not expect" (Matthew 24:44). Who is this "you"? His disciples (see also Matthew 24:4). These are the ones instructed to be ready. These, and not some unbelievers or Pharisees, were His audience here. And then He goes on to describe what is going to happen to the one that will not be found ready. To the one who at certain time said to himself "my master is delayed". I do not think that this servant said this from the first day. To say to himself "my Lord is delayed" starting then behaving the way described in the passage means that some time had first passed in which this servant did not behave this way. But then he said to himself "my master is delayed" and began *"to beat his fellow servants and to eat and drink with drunkards"*. He started in other words living like he had no Lord anymore. What happened then, or better what will happen when the Lord comes back? Here is the answer:

"the master of that servant will come on a day when he does not expect him and at an hour he does not know *and will cut him in pieces and put him with the hypocrites. In that place there will be weeping and gnashing of teeth."*

Wow! Cut him into pieces, because he did not end up well, though he most probably started well? That's exactly what the Lord says. Basically what He tells us is: pay attention, be alerted and make sure you are found faithful when I come. If we are found faithful we will be blessed and great would be our reward. But those who on the way will say to themselves "my Lord is delayed", starting living like the hypocrites, will, according to the above passage, also share the end of the hypocrites. And the Lord does not stop here. He further stretches His point - with 2 additional parables and another unparabolical passage, all one after the other. So let's move to the immediately next parable: the parable of the ten virgins.

## 3.2. THE PARABLE OF THE TEN VIRGINS

This we find in Matthew 25:1-13. There we read:

"Then the kingdom of heaven will be like ten virgins who took their lamps and went to meet the bridegroom. Five of them were foolish, and five were wise. For when the foolish took their lamps, they took no oil with them, but the wise took flasks of oil with their lamps. As the bridegroom was delayed, they all became drowsy and slept. But at midnight there was a cry, 'Here is the bridegroom! Come out to meet him.' Then all those virgins rose and trimmed their lamps. And the foolish said to the wise, 'Give us some of your oil, for our lamps are going out.' But the wise answered, saying, 'Since there will not be enough for us and for you, go rather to the dealers and buy for yourselves.' And while they were going to buy, the bridegroom came, and *those who were ready went in with him to the marriage feast, and the door was shut.* Afterward the other virgins came also, saying, 'Lord, lord, open to us. *But he answered, 'Truly, I say to you, I do not know you.'* Watch therefore, for you know neither the day nor the hour."

Concerning the lamps of the parable, Barnes says in his commentary:

"The "lamps" used on the marriage occasion were rather "torches" or "flambeaux." They were made by winding rags around pieces of iron or earthenware, *sometimes hollowed so as to contain oil,* and fastened to handles of wood. *These torches were dipped in oil,* and gave a large light." (emphasis added)

If he is right, this means that all ten girls initially had oil for their lamps. In any case, it is clear from the text that *all ten were, in the beginning, waiting for the Lord, waiting to meet the bridegroom.* But the five foolish ones did not take (additional) oil with them. Perhaps they expected that the Lord would come immediately and so they would not need it or they simply did not care. The five wise ones however, recognizing that they "know neither the time nor the hour" of the Lord's coming did not by any means want their lamps to go out. So they made the necessary provisions. The Lord finally came at midnight, when nobody expected Him. But the five foolish did not have oil. Their lamps were going out. When the Lord came they were not ready and they were not present at the marriage feast. When they came to the door, they found it closed and the Lord, instead of opening to them and welcoming them in, even though they were late, said to them: "Truly I say to you, I do not know you".

That the Lord said this parable to warn us, is obvious from the last verse of the passage where we read:

*"Watch therefore*, for *you* know neither the day nor the hour".

Again, this "you" is not some general audience or some Pharisees, but His very apostles and disciples (see the beginning of the teaching in Matthew 24:4). In other words what the Lord is telling us, His disciples, is: therefore, because you see what happened to the five unprepared ones, watch, be alerted. If this was not relevant to us, if we would enter into the Kingdom regardless of whether we are of those who believed but fell eventually away or of those who run the race to the end, abiding in the vine, then there would be no reason for the Lord to tell us this "Watch therefore". There would be in fact no reason to give us this parable. But the Lord, right at the end of His ministry (we are here two days before crucifixion) and speaking not to some general public but to His very own apostles and disciples, choose to give this warning. This in turn means that the danger of being found without oil, of being found no longer abiding in Him is real and real are also the consequences. People who are found in such a shape, will not hear the welcoming voice of the Master but rather what he said to the five virgins that had run out of oil: "Truly I say to you, I do not know you".

### 3.3. THE PARABLE OF THE TALENTS

The parable of the ten virgins is immediately followed by another parable with the same subject: that we ought to be watchful, serving the Lord and be focused on Him. The matter is very important, critical, and the whole of Matthew 25 is devoted to it. The second parable in this chapter and the third in the row is the parable of the talents. Let's read it, starting from the conclusion of the parable of the ten virgins.

Matthew 25:13-15
"Watch therefore, for you know neither the day nor the hour. "*For* it will be like a man going on a journey, who called his servants and entrusted to them his property. To one he gave five talents, to another two, to another one, to each according to his ability. Then he went away."

The word "for" that I have emphasized in bold, clearly links the parable of the talents to the parable of the ten virgins and especially to the conclusion of it i.e. that we should be watchful, because we know neither the day nor the hour of the Lord's coming. Then the Lord goes on to tell us that different talents were given to the different servants and the criterion was their ability. What we can say from this is that ALL the servants of the Lord, all those who have made Him Lord, have received gifts from Him, talents to be used for His purposes. They are *His* talents and they were given for *His* purposes. We can also see that not everyone received the same. One received five, one received two and one received one talent. The determining factor of how much each one received was, according to the passage, his ability, his capacity to increase what he received. Let's see now what the servants did with what they received:

Matthew 25:16-18
"He who had received the five talents went at once and traded with them, and he made five talents more. So also he who had the two talents made two talents more. But he who had received the one talent went and dug in the ground and *hid his master's money.*"

The first and the second servant did what was expected of them: they went out and increased what was given to them, making it in fact double. But the third servant went on and hid what was given to him. Pay attention here: he did not consume it. He did not lose it. Instead he did *nothing* with it. He was in other words, fruitless for his master. Let's now see the reaction of the Lord:

34

Matthew 25:19-30

"Now after a long time the master of those servants came and settled accounts with them. And he who had received the five talents came forward, bringing five talents more, saying, 'Master, you delivered to me five talents; here I have made five talents more.' His master said to him, 'Well done, good and faithful servant. You have been faithful over a little; I will set you over much. Enter into the joy of your master.' And he also who had the two talents came forward, saying, 'Master, you delivered to me two talents; here I have made two talents more.' His master said to him, 'Well done, good and faithful servant. You have been faithful over a little; I will set you over much. Enter into the joy of your master.' He also who had received the one talent came forward, saying, 'Master, I knew you to be a hard man, reaping where you did not sow, and gathering where you scattered no seed, so I was afraid, and I went and hid your talent in the ground. Here you have what is yours.' But his master answered him, 'You wicked and slothful servant! You knew that I reap where I have not sown and gather where I scattered no seed? Then you ought to have invested my money with the bankers, and at my coming I should have received what was my own with interest. So take the talent from him and give it to him who has the ten talents. For to everyone who has will more be given, and he will have an abundance. But from the one who has not, even what he has will be taken away. And cast the worthless servant into the outer darkness. In that place there will be weeping and gnashing of teeth.'"

The first and second servant got their reward for the multiplication of what the Lord had given to them. But the third servant? The Lord calls him a slothful, lazy servant. This servant did nothing. He did not harm but he did not do any good either. He was completely useless. What was finally the end of this fruitless servant? The last verse of the parable tells us:

"cast the worthless servant into the outer darkness. In that place there will be weeping and gnashing of teeth"

I was watching a children's cartoon recently and its subject was this very parable. Once the film came to the last servant and his fate, they changed what the Lord said and instead of what we just read, they showed the two other servants giving from what they had earned to the slothful servant, so that at the end "everybody was happy". It is obvious that some feel uncomfortable with some of the things the Lord said. So they change it. Let us not follow them. In contrast let us take these passages at heart and answer to the call of alertness they are offering.

Doing – with whatever mistakes and failures - the will of God, bearing fruit for the Lord, is not optional, something that a Christian could opt to do, if he would like to, but if he does not do it, never mind: he may only miss some rewards but still make it into the Kingdom, because of that confession of faith he made once upon a time. It is not really like this. Instead, striving, with whatever failures and shortcomings, to do the will of God, doing and not just hearing the Word of God is what the Word asks us to do. As James tells us:

James 1:22-25
*"But be doers of the word, and not hearers only, deceiving yourselves. For if anyone is a hearer of the word and not a doer, he is like a man who looks intently at his natural face in a mirror. For he looks at himself and goes away and at once forgets what he was like. But the one who looks into the perfect law, the law of liberty, and perseveres, being no hearer who forgets but a doer who acts, he will be blessed in his doing. "*

And as the Lord plainly said in Matthew 7:21-27:
*"Not everyone who says to me, 'Lord, Lord,' will enter the kingdom of heaven, but the one who does the will of my Father who is in heaven. On that day many will say to me, 'Lord, Lord, did we not prophesy in your name, and cast out demons in your name, and do many mighty works in your name?' And then will I declare to them, 'I never knew you; depart from me, you workers of lawlessness.'*

"Everyone then who hears these words of mine and *does them* will be like a wise man who built his house on the rock. And the rain fell, and the floods came, and the winds blew and beat on that house, but it did not fall, because it had been founded on the rock. And everyone who hears these words of mine and *does not do them* will be like a foolish man who built his house on the sand. And the rain fell, and the floods came, and the winds blew and beat against that house, and it fell, and great was the fall of it."

"Not everyone who says to me, 'Lord, Lord,' will enter the kingdom of heaven, *but the one who does the will of my Father who is in heaven*". Could it be any plainer? I repeat that this does not mean that we are faultless not it means that we are walking perfectly. What it does mean though is that we are running with patience the race of faith, looking unto Jesus the author and the finisher of our faith (Hebrews 12:1-2). It means that we are on the move following Jesus, trying, yes with mistakes but with the power of Christ that is greater than everything, to do the will of God, thus bringing, as we move united with Him, the desired fruit. For some this may be five talents and for others two. The Lord does not criticize the one who made two, instead of five, additional talents. In contrast He congratulates him. He brought fruit for his Lord according to what was given to him. The one who is condemned is the one who was fruitless. The one who instead of working His Lord worked other lords (we always serve a lord). His behavior had indeed consequences and in fact very heavy ones:

"cast the worthless servant into the outer darkness. In that place there will be weeping and gnashing of teeth"

### 3.4. "FOR I WAS HUNGRY AND YOU GAVE ME NO FOOD, I WAS THIRSTY AND YOU GAVE ME NO DRINK"

Matthew 25 does not end with the parable of the talents, but it is immediately followed by the below unparabolical passage, which is directly connected to the three parables we previously read:

Matthew 25:31-46
"When the Son of Man comes in his glory, and all the angels with him, then he will sit on his glorious throne. Before him will be gathered all the nations, and he will separate people one from another as a shepherd separates the sheep from the goats. And he will place the sheep on his right, but the goats on the left. Then the King will say to those on his right, 'Come, you who are blessed by my Father, inherit the kingdom prepared for you from the foundation of the world. For I was hungry and you gave me food, I was thirsty and you gave me drink, I was a stranger and you welcomed me, I was naked and you clothed me, I was sick and you visited me, I was in prison and you came to me. 'Then the righteous will answer him, saying, 'Lord, when did we see you hungry and feed you, or thirsty and give you drink? And when did we see you a stranger and welcome you, or naked and clothe you? And when did we see you sick or in prison and visit you?' And the King will answer them, 'Truly, I say to you, as you did it to one of the least of these my brothers, you did it to me.' "Then he will say to those on his left, 'Depart from me, you cursed, into the eternal fire prepared for the devil and his angels. For I was hungry and you gave me no food, I was thirsty and you gave me no drink, I was a stranger and you did not welcome me, naked and you did not clothe me, sick and in prison and you did not visit me.' Then they also will answer, saying, 'Lord, when did we see you hungry or thirsty or a stranger or naked or sick or in prison, and did not minister to you?' Then he will answer them, saying, 'Truly, I say to you, as you did not do it to one of the least of these, you did not do it to me.' And these will go away into eternal punishment, but the righteous into eternal life.'"

Some are quick to dismiss the above passage as referring to others and not to us, as we are saved by grace through faith and not by works. I would happily accept – and it is true that I did it for years – this reasoning, if I did not see the following problems with it:

To whom was the Lord speaking when He said the above words as well as the three parables of Matthew 24 and 25 we read? This is very obvious from the context. The teaching of the Lord started as an answer to the following question of the disciples:

Matthew 24:3
"As he sat on the Mount of Olives, *the disciples came to him privately*, saying, "Tell us, when will these things be, and what will be the sign of your coming and of the end of the age?"

Then after He tells them about the false christs, the false prophets, the abomination of desolation etc., He says:

Matthew 24:36-39, 42-43
"But concerning that day and hour no one knows, not even the angels of heaven, nor the Son, but the Father only. For as were the days of Noah, so will be the coming of the Son of Man. For as in those days before the flood they were eating and drinking, marrying and giving in marriage, until the day when Noah entered the ark, and they were unaware until the flood came and swept them all away, so will be the coming of the Son of Man. ....
*Therefore, stay awake, for you do not know on what day your Lord is coming.* But know this, that if the master of the house had known in what part of the night the thief was coming, he would have stayed awake and would not have let his house be broken into. *Therefore you also must be ready, for the Son of Man is coming at an hour you do not expect.*"

"Therefore, stay awake, for you do not know on what day your Lord is coming". Who are those that are to stay awake, to be alerted? His disciples. And then the Lord proceeds by giving several examples which all refer to one and the same case: *how somebody waiting for the Lord to come, should behave during the time of His absence.* Are we not exactly these people? If we are not these people, then who is? To say it differently, if we exclude ourselves from these words of Christ which He said to His disciples, then there is nobody else to whom these words could refer to. This is the basic reason which makes me believe that these words of the Lord do not refer to some others but to me personally. Also see the timing these words were said. This is stated explicitly in Matthew 26:1-2:

Matthew 26:1-2
"When Jesus had finished all these sayings, he said to his disciples, "You know *that after two days the Passover is coming, and the Son of Man will be delivered up to be crucified."*

These were teachings delivered to his disciples right at the close of the Lord's ministry, two days before the crucifixion. He did not give them only for information but for application! Furthermore, what Jesus said above is not at all unique. See here what John says in his epistle:

1 John 3:16-18
"By this we know love, that he laid down his life for us, and we ought to lay down our lives for the brothers. *But if anyone has the world's goods and sees his brother in need, yet closes his heart against him, how does God's love abide in him?* Little children, let us not love in word or talk but in deed and in truth."

James uses the same example of 1 John 3:16-18 and makes it even louder:

James 2:14-17
"What good is it, my brothers, if someone says he has faith but does not have works? Can that faith save him? If a brother or sister is poorly clothed and lacking in daily food, and one of you says to them, "Go in peace, be warmed and filled," without giving them the things needed for the body, what good is that? *So also faith by itself, if it does not have works, is dead."*

Whether we are truly Christ's followers is shown very simply by whether or not we follow His Word, doing - yes with mistake and failures (I repeat: we are not yet perfect but we are running towards it (Philippians 3:12)) - what this Word says. As the Lord said, not everybody that calls Him Lord Lord will enter into the Kingdom but those who do the will of His Father. It is indeed faith that saves but true faith, and such faith is manifested in doing the will of God, the works that God has prepared for us. And just to avoid any misunderstanding: for many of these works we do not need any special revelation. They are written plainly in His Word. Here are some:

"I was hungry and you gave me food, I was thirsty and you gave me drink, I was a stranger and you welcomed me, I was naked and you clothed me, I was sick and you visited me, I was in prison and you came to me. 'Then the righteous will answer him, saying, 'Lord, when did we see you hungry and feed you, or thirsty and give you drink? And when did we see you a stranger and welcome you, or naked and clothe you? And when did we see you sick or in prison and visit you?' And the King will answer them, 'Truly, I say to you, as you did it to one of the least of these my brothers, you did it to me.'"

And James 1:27
"Religion that is pure and undefiled before God, the Father, is this: to visit orphans and widows in their affliction, and to keep oneself unstained from the world."

## 3.5 THE PARABLE OF THE DEBTOR OF THE TEN THOUSAND TALENTS

We find this parable in Matthew 18:23-35. There we read:

"Therefore the kingdom of heaven may be compared to a king who wished to settle accounts with his servants. When he began to settle, one was brought to him who owed him ten thousand talents. And since he could not pay, his master ordered him to be sold, with his wife and children and all that he had, and payment to be made. So the servant fell on his knees, imploring him, 'Have patience with me, and I will pay you everything.' And out of pity for him, the master of that servant released him and forgave him the debt. But when that same servant went out, he found one of his fellow servants who owed him a hundred denarii, and seizing him, he began to choke him, saying, 'Pay what you owe.' So his fellow servant fell down and pleaded with him, 'Have patience with me, and I will pay you.' He refused and went and put him in prison until he should pay the debt. When his fellow servants saw what had taken place, they were greatly distressed, and they went and reported to their master all that had taken place. Then his master summoned him and said to him, 'You wicked servant! I forgave you all that debt because you pleaded with me. And should not you have had mercy on your fellow servant, as I had mercy on you?' And in anger his master delivered him to the jailers, until he should pay all his debt. *So also my heavenly Father will do to every one of you, if you do not forgive your brother from your heart.*"

Ten thousand talents is a *huge* amount. Nobody could ever earn this amount of money. And yet this huge debt is what this servant owed. And do you know what happened? His Lord forgave him this debt. This is *grace*! Grace means unmerited favor. And this is exactly what this Master, who is a type of God, did: upon the pleading of his servant, he forgave him and removed this huge debt. This servant was now free! He was forgiven! Also note that he did not do anything to earn forgiveness of the debt other than pleading with the master. Up to here I believe all of us would agree that this is a perfect picture of me and you. What happened to this servant, the grace and compassion that was shown to him, is the same grace and compassion that was shown to us by God. As Ephesians 2:1-9 says, speaking about us:

Ephesians 2.1-9

*"And you were dead in the trespasses and sins in which you once walked,* following the course of this world, following the prince of the power of the air, the spirit that is now at work in the sons of disobedience — among whom we all once lived in the passions of our flesh, carrying out the desires of the body and the mind, and were by nature children of wrath, like the rest of mankind. *But God, being rich in mercy, because of the great love with which he loved us, even when we were dead in our trespasses, made us alive together with Christ — by grace you have been saved — and raised us up with him and seated us with him in the heavenly places in Christ Jesus,* so that in the coming ages he might show the immeasurable riches of his grace in kindness toward us in Christ Jesus. For by grace you have been saved through faith. And this is not your own doing; it is the gift of God, not a result of works, so that no one may boast."

Our debt was huge. We were dead in trespasses and sins. We were enemies of God and sons of disobedience. And what happened? We repented and believed. We bowed down like that servant and asked the King to forgive us. And He did! This is called grace. By grace we were saved. And so was that servant: by grace he was saved from his huge debt. There were no works, nothing me, you or that servant could do to pay that debt. Only grace could do this. So salvation is by faith through grace and cannot be earned in exchange for our works as no works could ever repay our huge debt. I think up to here, so far so good. But the Lord does not stop here!

He looks at what the servant did: in spite of the huge debt of which he was forgiven, he denied to forgive his fellow servant the tiny debt he owed him. The servant was forgiven but he did not walk as forgiven. *Now would the King be just if He did not make any judgment here?* No he would not. In contrast he would be completely unjust. And yet this is what many expect God to do with them: they expect Him to forgive them, but not to judge them when they insist in not walking as forgiven. When the Lord judged the servant and reinstated the huge dead that was originally forgiven, was He graceless? No. His grace was manifested when He originally forgave the servant of his huge debt. But seeing that this servant was not at all walking as forgiven but had taken advantage of his freedom pressuring his co-servants and asking "justice" to be done about their negligible debt to him, justice had to be applied to him too! So do not misunderstand grace and justice. God is both: He is both full of grace and full of justice. If we repent from the heart we receive grace. However, if we are unforgiving, essentially requesting judgment against those who supposedly wronged us, then judgment will be applied but it will start from us! Our Lord leaves no space for misunderstanding:

"'You wicked servant! I forgave you all that debt because you pleaded with me. And should not you have had mercy on your fellow servant, as I had mercy on you?' And in anger his master delivered him to the jailers, until he should pay all his debt. *So also my heavenly Father will do to every one of you, if you do not forgive your brother from your heart.*"

And again in the Lord's prayer:

Matthew 6:12
"And forgive us our debts, *as we forgive our debtors.*"

This He explained further in verses 14-15:
"For if you forgive men their trespasses, your heavenly Father will also forgive you. *But if you do not forgive men their trespasses, neither will your Father forgive your trespasses.*"

That God is not just full of kindness and goodness but also full of righteousness with the respective severity that goes along, is summarized in an excellent way by Paul in Romans 11:22, when he says:

"Note then *the kindness and the severity of God*: severity toward those who have fallen, but God's kindness to you, provided you continue in his kindness. Otherwise you too will be cut off."

There is the kindness of God and that is what we will have if we continue walking the narrow path of faith, abiding in Christ, in the One who paid the price for us. But if we do not do this and we do not continue in His kindness, if in other words we choose, like that servant, to walk like we were not forgiven from the sins and the trespasses in which we were dead, then there is no kindness to be expected but severity. God is both and it is obvious that we choose what we get.

## 3.6. "TO THE ONE WHO OVERCOMES"

There are some Bibles that have the words of Jesus marked in red. If you have one of these Bibles, you will observe that after the gospels you see very little in red color in the Acts and the epistles, perhaps all in all a dozen verses. Though the Acts and the epistles have as their author the same Holy Spirit as the gospels, Jesus is not speaking in the first person there. This however changes in Revelation, the last book of the Bible. There Jesus speaks again in the first person and in this section I would like to point out certain things from the second and the third chapter of Revelation. These chapters contain letters addressed to seven churches of Minor Asia. Jesus Himself dictated these letters to the apostle John, commanding him to write them down and send them to these churches, together with the whole book. It is surprising however how little attention these epistles of Jesus receive. One theory I have heard is that these epistles of Jesus together with the whole book of Revelation do not really refer to us but to future believers and that they are going to understand it, implying implicitly that we can safely ignore this book or consider it as something "just for our information". In the third appendix of this book I am giving the reasons why I believe this view is wrong.

Now going on to the letters themselves, what I want to point out here and I believe is relevant for this study, is the following fact: in all seven letters the Lord ends with a promise to the one who *overcomes*. Let's read these promises:

Revelation 2:7
*"To him who overcomes* I will give to eat from the tree of life, which is in the midst of the Paradise of God."

Revelation 2:11
*"He who overcomes* shall not be hurt by the second death."

Revelation 2:17
*"To him who overcomes* I will give some of the hidden manna to eat. And I will give him a white stone, and on the stone a new name written which no one knows except him who receives it."

Revelation 2:26-28
"And *he who overcomes, and keeps My works until the end,* to him I will give power over the nations– 'He shall rule them with a rod of iron; They shall be dashed to pieces like the potter's vessels' – as I also have received from My Father; "and I will give him the morning star."

Revelation 3:5
*"He who overcomes* shall be clothed in white garments, and I will not blot out his name from the Book of Life; but I will confess his name before My Father and before His angels."

Revelation 3:12
*"He who overcomes,* I will make him a pillar in the temple of My God, and he shall go out no more. I will write on him the name of My God and the name of the city of My God, the New Jerusalem, which comes down out of heaven from My God. And I will write on him My new name."

And Revelation 3:21
*"To him who overcomes* I will grant to sit with Me on My throne, as I also overcame and sat down with My Father on His throne."

It is amazing all that is promised to the one who overcomes; to the one who perseveres to the end, who keeps the works and the words of Jesus even unto the point of death. However, many today believe that they do not need to overcome anything. They believe that all was done and dusted for them in time past, at that one moment of faith. Essentially and according to their view the race of faith not only started at the moment we believed, but also finished at that moment. But if this was really so then there would be no reason for Jesus to speak about those who overcome. For speaking about it not only means that there is a need to overcome but also that there will be some who will *not* overcome and to them the above promises will not apply.

Just to take the promise of Revelation 3:5 as an example:

*"He who overcomes* shall be clothed in white garments, and I will not blot out his name from the Book of Life; but I will confess his name before My Father and before His angels."

If we overcome our names will not be blotted out from the Book of Life, Jesus promised. But this also means that if we do not overcome our names will indeed be blotted out. The Book of life is a register of those who are to live forever (see Philippians 4:3). Those in it will have eternal life and enter into the new Jerusalem (Revelation 21:27) but those who will not be in it will end up in the lake of fire (Revelation 20:15). To say it in another way: eternal life have those and only those who are in the book of life. And as is obvious from what Jesus says, the book of life does not only accept new entries. It also accepts removals of entries, for those who do not overcome i.e. those who retreat, stepping back. Therefore, being in the book of life, does not guarantee that we will be in that book forever. Whoever draws back, falling away from the faith without repentance (wherever this repentance is still available – see later our discussion on Hebrews 6), whoever does not overcome, he will not be found at the end in the book of life. I know that many people are not used to hear such things but this is the simple truth which I see in the Word and personally I am not willing to ignore it nor am I willing to device ways to explain it away.

## 3.7. CONCLUSION

To conclude this chapter, it is obvious that our Lord in no way believed in an unfruitful faith. His sayings pave the way for the right understanding of what it means to believe in Jesus or have faith in Jesus. This is in no way only a confession but, as the apostle Paul taught (see the coming chapter), a race to be run and a fight to be fought. There is no question that for Him, abiding in Him, was not something optional but mandatory and in case some did not abide in Him then they would not enter into the Kingdom. Unfortunately though, many have chosen to ignore this, believing that what only matters is to start in the faith. Of course it is important to start in the faith (you cannot finish something unless you first start it), but I would say that even more important is to both start *and* finish in the faith, staying in the vine, in Christ, till the end and putting aside whatever may want to move you away from it.

**4**

## "FAITH WORKING THROUGH LOVE"

Now, having seeing the above and before we continue with additional material, I would like to make a parenthesis here and say some things concerning love. I believe that this is necessary as the works of faith the New Testament refers to are works whose motivating force is love. Galatians 5:5 summarizes this excellently when it says:

Galatians 5:6
For in Christ Jesus neither circumcision nor uncircumcision counts for anything, but only *faith working through love*.

Here we have everything in one phrase: Faith, love, works! None of these can stand alone. Works without faith have no validity. Without benefit are also works not motivated by love. As Paul says in 1 Corinthians 13:1-3:

"If I speak in the tongues of men and of angels, but have not love, I am a noisy gong or a clanging cymbal. And if I have prophetic powers, and understand all mysteries and all knowledge, and if I have all faith, so as to remove mountains, but have not love, I am nothing. *If I give away all I have, and if I deliver up my body to be burned, but have not love, I gain nothing.*"

And then he moves on giving what exactly love does and what it does not:

1 Corinthians 13:4-8, 13
"Love is patient and kind; love does not envy or boast; it is not arrogant or rude. It does not insist on its own way; it is not irritable or resentful; it does not rejoice at wrongdoing, but rejoices with the truth. Love bears all things, believes all things, hopes all things, endures all things. Love never ends. .. So now faith, hope, and love abide, these three; but the greatest of these is love."

It is obvious that real love is not just a nice feeling.

Now as the works without love as motivator are without gain, so also love without works is not real love. As John tells us:

1 John 3:16-18
"By this we know love, that he laid down his life for us, and we ought to lay down our lives for the brothers. But if anyone has the world's goods and sees his brother in need, yet closes his heart against him, how does God's love abide in him? *Little children, let us not love in word or talk but in deed and in truth.*"

Love is true love when it becomes action, when it is working, in deed and in truth.

Therefore we see that faith, works and love are not things that can really exist as stand alones separately from each other. Faith without works is dead tells us James (James 2:17) and works without love are without gain tells us Paul. Furthermore, love without works is not true love tells us John. What is then true faith? It is a faith that has it all. It is very plainly: "*faith working through love*".

# 5

## THE WARNINGS OF THE EPISTLES

Moving on in our study we will now pass to the epistles.

### 5.1. ROMANS 11:22 – GOD'S KINDNESS, IF YOU CONTINUE IN HIS KINDNESS

To start let's go to Romans 11:19-22. There we read about Israel and those of us who believe:

"Then you will say, "Branches were broken off so that I might be grafted in." That is true. They [he means Israel] were broken off because of their unbelief, but you stand fast through faith. So do not become proud, but fear. For if God did not spare the natural branches, neither will he spare you. Note then the kindness and the severity of God: severity toward those who have fallen, *but God's kindness to you, **provided** you continue in His kindness. Otherwise you too will be cut off.*"

This passage refers to people who "stand fast through faith". For such people, for those of us who stand fast through faith, the kindness of God is upon us. But this is not unconditional: the word "provided", or "if", as other translations have it, clearly

51

introduces a condition, an "if statement". What is the condition? That we will continue in His kindness. If we abandon this kindness and no longer continue with God, then the answer the Word gives is clear: *we too will be cut off.*

That there are limits after which one is no longer in the faith, is clear also by what Paul says in 2 Corinthians 13:5:

2 Corinthians 13:5
"Examine yourselves, *to see whether you are in the faith. Test yourselves.* Or do you not realize this about yourselves, that Jesus Christ is in you? — unless indeed you fail to meet the test!"

From this it is evident that it can happen that a Christian is no longer in the faith i.e. he has implicitly or explicitly abandoned it. If there was no such case, there would also be no reason for Paul to tell us to examine ourselves whether we are really in the faith. Perhaps that is why we find him and Barnabas in Acts 14:21-22 doing the following:

"And when they had preached the gospel to that city, and had taught many, they returned again to Lystra, and to Iconium, and Antioch, confirming the souls of the disciples, *and exhorting them to continue in the faith,* and that we must through much tribulation enter into the kingdom of God."

There would be no point in the apostles exhorting the believers *to continue in the faith,* if there was no possibility to *discontinue in the faith.* It is therefore possible for a believer to discontinue in the faith, to discontinue in God's kindness. What will happen in that case? Romans 11:22 gave us the answer in no unclear terms: he will be cut off.

Jesus said exactly the same about those who no longer abide in Him:

John 15:1-2, 6
"I am the true vine, and my Father is the vinedresser. Every branch in me that does not bear fruit *he takes away* [i.e. "cuts off"] … "*If anyone does not abide in me he is thrown away like a branch and withers; and the branches are gathered, thrown into the fire, and burned."*

So being "cut off", or "taken away" is not something impossible, as various people would have us believe, but a serious possibility that will materialize for whoever no longer abides in the vine, according to John's words, or discontinues in the faith, discontinues in His kindness, according to Paul's words.

## 5.2. COLOSSIANS 1:21-23 – "HOLY AND BLAMELESS, IF YOU CONTINUE IN THE FAITH"

Moving on, in Colossians 1:21-23 we read:

Colossians 1:21-23
"And you, who once were alienated and enemies in your mind by wicked works, yet now He has reconciled in the body of His flesh through death, to present you holy, and blameless, and above reproach in His sight — *if indeed you continue in the faith, grounded and steadfast, and are not moved away from the hope of the gospel* which you heard, which was preached to every creature under heaven, of which I, Paul, became a minister."

Christ has indeed reconciled us to God in the body of His flesh through death, to present us holy and blameless. But this is not unconditional, as there is again an "IF" here, a condition which must be kept in order for these wonderful truths to become a full reality to us in the day of the Lord. What is this condition? Here it is: "*if indeed you continue in the faith, grounded and steadfast, and are not moved away from the hope of the gospel*". Again see this "continue in the faith". We saw in Romans 11, that if we do not continue in His kindness we will be cut off. The same we see also here: if we do not continue in the faith i.e. if we discontinue in the faith, then we are *not* going to be counted among those whom He will present as "holy, blameless and above reproach".

As also the epistle to the Hebrews tells us:

Hebrews 12:14
"Strive for peace with everyone, *and for the holiness without which no one will see the Lord.*"

Only holy people are going to see the Lord and have eternal life. And only Christ can present us as such! But when? "*If indeed we continue in the faith, grounded and steadfast, and are not moved away from the hope of the gospel*".

## 5.3. THE RACE OF FAITH: THE EXAMPLE OF PAUL

That faith is rather a race to be run and a fight to be fought, is obvious from what Paul said and instructed. As he said to Timothy:

1 Timothy 6:11-12
"But as for you, O man of God, flee these things. Pursue righteousness, godliness, faith, love, steadfastness, gentleness. *Fight the good fight of the faith. Take hold of the eternal life to which you were called* and about which you made the good confession in the presence of many witnesses."

From this instruction, two things become apparent:

1. Faith IS indeed a fight. "Fight the good fight of the faith" says Paul.

2. We were called unto eternal life, but we also have to take hold of it. The Greek word translated as "take hold" here is the word

"epilavou" and means "catch, lay hold on, take" (Strong's dictionary). We have been called to eternal life but this does not mean that we have "caught" it yet. We are running towards it.

But Paul did not only give instructions. First of all he applied these to himself. As he says:

Philippians 3:8-15
"Indeed, I count everything as loss because of the surpassing worth of knowing Christ Jesus my Lord. For his sake I have suffered the loss of all things and count them as rubbish, in order that I may gain Christ and be found in him, not having a righteousness of my own that comes from the law, but that which comes through faith in Christ, the righteousness from God that depends on faith — that I may know him and the power of his resurrection, and may share his sufferings, becoming like him in his death, that by any means possible I may attain the resurrection from the dead. *Not that I have already obtained this or am already perfect, but I press on if that I may apprehend that for which also I am apprehended of Christ Jesus.* Brothers, I do not consider that I have made it my own. But one thing I do: forgetting what lies behind and straining forward to what lies ahead, *I press on toward the goal for the prize of the upward call of God in Christ Jesus.* Let those of us who are mature think this way, and if in anything you think otherwise, God will reveal that also to you."

And again in 1 Corinthians 9:24-27
"Do you not know that in a race all the runners run, but only one receives the prize? *So run that you may obtain it.* Every athlete exercises self-control in all things. They do it to receive a perishable wreath, but we an imperishable. So I do not run aimlessly; I do not box as one beating the air. *But I discipline my body and keep it under control, lest after preaching to others I myself should be disqualified.*"

As Paul said concerning himself: "Not that I have already obtained this or am already perfect, but I press on if that I may apprehend that for which also I am apprehended of Christ Jesus. ... I press on toward the goal for the prize of the upward call of God in Christ Jesus". And again: "Brothers, I do not consider that I have made it my own." The picture we get from Paul is not the picture of a Christian who has achieved his aim and is now sitting back. In contrast, the picture we get is that of an athlete running towards his goal, "that by any means possible" he may attain it. It is the picture of a good fighter who does not box as one beating the air, but fights having his eyes on victory, on the prize waiting for him.

Only at the end of his life Paul said the following:

2 Timothy 4:6-8
"For I am already being poured out as a drink offering, and the time of my departure has come. *I have fought the good fight, I have finished the race, I have kept the faith.* Henceforth there is laid up for me the crown of righteousness, which the Lord, the righteous judge, will award to me on that Day, and not only to me but also to all who have loved His appearing."

Faith is for Paul something that needs keeping. "I have kept the faith" he said. Obviously then faith is not something static, something which once you are in, it is a done deal: you can sit back and reach the end automatically. In contrast faith is for Paul a good fight to be fought and a race to be run. The eternal life is not something we have already caught. It is something we have been called to and we are running to take hold of it, to set our hands on it.

May all of us be able at the end of our life to say what Paul said: "*I have fought the good fight, I have finished the race, I have kept the faith*". May none of us consider that he received the prize when Paul himself would not think this for himself but only at the end. Let us all run the race of faith as he did and let us imitate him, as he also tells us to do (1 Corinthians 11:1).

## 5.4. HEBREWS 12:22-25: "WE SHALL NOT ESCAPE IF WE TURN AWAY FROM HIM"

We will now go to the epistle of Hebrews, where many warnings are found. Let's start from Hebrews 12:22-25. There we read:

"But you have come to Mount Zion and to the city of the living God, the heavenly Jerusalem, to an innumerable company of angels, to the general assembly and church of the firstborn who are registered in heaven, to God the Judge of all, to the spirits of just men made perfect, to Jesus the Mediator of the new covenant, and to the blood of sprinkling that speaks better things than that of Abel. *See that you do not refuse Him who speaks. For if they did not escape who refused him who spoke on earth, much more shall we not escape if we turn away from Him who speaks from heaven*"

The epistle to the Hebrews, as every other epistle is addressed to believers. When the word "you" therefore is used, this can only refer to believers. And indeed only to believers could the following phrase apply: "you have come to Mount Zion and to the city of the living God, the heavenly Jerusalem". No unbeliever has come or will ever come into the city of the living God, unless of course he becomes a believer. The author is clearly addressing believers. Then, using the example of the Israelites and how they perished, he warns his audience, telling them: "See that you do not refuse Him who speaks. For if they did not escape who refused him who spoke on earth, much more shall we not escape if we turn away from Him who speaks from heaven" From this warning two things become once again apparent:

i) a believer, somebody who has come to the city of the living God, can turn away, can refuse God.

ii) if he does this, then the faith he once had – but he has no more – will not really make him escape, save him.

Also the example given is telling: all Israelites started in one accord for the promised land. But on the way almost everyone, turned away, rejecting God and His plan. Did God allow them to enter the promised Land, for which they had started to go and into which God had originally called them to enter? No, He did not. Those who refused Him on the way died in the wilderness. This is not an analogy that I give, but an analogy that the Word of God gives concerning those who decide to turn away from God. As the Israelites, who turned away did not enter into the promised land, so also we, though we have been called to eternal life, we will not escape, we will not enter into the promised Kingdom, if on the way we turn away from God.

## 5.5. HEBREWS 4:1-3, 9-12: "STRIVE TO ENTER THE REST OF GOD"

Moving to the next passage, from Hebrews 4 this time, we read:

"Therefore, while the promise of entering his rest still stands, *let us fear lest any of you should seem to have failed to reach it.* For good news came to us just as to them, but the message they heard did not benefit them, because they were not united by faith with those who listened. *For we who have believed enter that rest*, as he has said, "As I swore in my wrath, 'They shall not enter my rest,' although his works were finished from the foundation of the world. ...So then, there remains a Sabbath rest for the people of God, for whoever has entered God's rest has also rested from his works as God did from his. *Let us therefore strive to enter that rest, so that no one may fall by the same sort of disobedience.* For the word of God is living and active, sharper than any two-edged sword, piercing to the division of soul and/ of spirit, of joints and of marrow, and discerning the thoughts and intentions of the heart. "

Entering the rest of God, which I take it to be an alternative expression for entering the Kingdom of God, being saved, living eternally, is something designed for those of us "who have believed". This is the plan, the design of God for every believer. And this is exactly what will happen, unless somebody falls by disobeying God, refusing Him, turning away from Him, like the Israelites did. That is why the writer is saying: *"Let us therefore strive to enter that rest, so that no one may fall by the same sort of disobedience"*. It is interesting to look at the Greek word translated as "strive" here: this is the word "spoudazo" which means "to make effort, be prompt or earnest:  do (give) diligence, be diligent, endeavor, labor, study" (Strong's dictionary). We are to strive to enter into the rest of God. From this it is clear that entering the rest of God is neither something guaranteed nor something that happens automatically, once and for all, when one first believes. In contrast it is something we need to give diligence, in order to enter. This is what those of the second and third category of the parable of the sower did not do and as a result the seed of the Word never gave fruit. In contrast to them, the picture we get from Hebrews fits perfectly with the picture of the athlete Paul gave us previously in 1 Corinthians 9:24-27:

1 Corinthians 9:24-27
"Do you not know that in a race all the runners run, but only one receives the prize? *So run that you may obtain it. Every athlete exercises self-control in all things. They do it to receive a perishable wreath, but we an imperishable.* So I do not run aimlessly; I do not box as one beating the air. But I discipline my body and keep it under control, lest after preaching to others I myself should be disqualified."

The true believer tries to make good of his faith, striving to enter into the rest of God, practicing his faith, yes perhaps with failures, but not giving up. May we all do this and keep doing this to the end.

## 5.6. HEBREWS 6:4-9 – THOSE WHO BECAME PARTAKERS OF THE HOLY SPIRIT AND FELL AWAY

Continuing in Hebrews we read:

Hebrews 6:4-9
"For it is impossible for those who were once enlightened, and have tasted the heavenly gift, and have become partakers of the Holy Spirit, and have tasted the good word of God and the powers of the age to come, *if they fall away*, to renew them again to repentance, since they crucify again for themselves the Son of God, and put Him to an open shame. For the earth which drinks in the rain that often comes upon it, and bears herbs useful for those by whom it is cultivated, receives blessing from God; but if it bears thorns and briers, it is rejected and near to being cursed, whose end is to be burned. Though we speak in this way, yet in your case, beloved, we feel sure of better things — things that belong to salvation."

Three questions that one may ask concerning this passage:

i) does this passage speak about believers? This I believe is obvious, as it speaks about people who "have tasted the heavenly gift, and have become partakers of the holy spirit and have tasted the good word of God and the powers of the age to come". Can unbelievers or pretenders –who deceive others but not God – be for example partakers of the holy spirit? No, they cannot. Therefore, it is clear that the passage is addressing believers.

ii) Does this passage imply that people - who "were once enlightened, and have tasted the heavenly gift, and have become partakers of the Holy Spirit, and have tasted the good word of God and the powers of the age to come" - can "fall away", drop out? Yes, this exactly is what the text says.

iii) What will happen to those who fall away? Their end is resembled to the end of the earth that "bears thorns and briers,

60

and it is rejected and near to being cursed, *whose end is to be burned"*.

This again is a rather strong warning for those of us who have started the race of faith: starting the race is a great thing. But we also need to run it till the end. To fall away from the faith, to turn back abandoning the race, to abandon Christ the vine, is something that none of us should ever choose to do.

Now the passage makes clear that it is *impossible* "for those who were once enlightened, and have tasted the heavenly gift, and have become partakers of the Holy Spirit, and have tasted the good word of God and the powers of the age to come, if they fall away, to renew them again to repentance". In other words there is no way of return for such people. And as reason the passage gives the following:

*"since they crucify again for themselves the Son of God, and put Him to an open shame."*

It is my opinion that most of the cases of backsliding can be forgiven, when there is true repentance and return. However this case here is something different. "It is *impossible*", the passage says, that these people renew themselves again to repentance. I would not say that I understand 100% the reason that is given and I would not want to say things that the text does not clearly say. However, what the text does clearly say is that their act would be equal to crucifying the Lord again and putting Him to open shame. In other words with their example not only it would be like they themselves took part in the crucifixion but also they would demonstrate that he was supposedly worthy to be crucified. And this would not happen in ignorance but by people that had known the Lord and His goodness[3]. In my opinion we do not

---

[3] Those who originally crucified the Lord, crying in front of Pilate "crucify Him, crucify Him", did it in ignorance (Acts 3:14-21). The door of repentance was open to them. But those of Hebrews 6 are something else. These ones had they rejected the Lord, they would have done it not in ignorance but *in full knowledge* and after

have here "simply" a move to a wrong path but a public denial, an open rejection, of Christ by people who "were enlightened, and have tasted the heavenly gift, and have become partakers of the Holy Spirit, and have tasted the good word of God and the powers of the age to come". For such a behavior there is no way for repentance.

Perhaps the public renunciation of Christ is something whose motives may be difficult to be understood by those of us living in the "secure" and without particular persecution western societies. But it was not like this in the first century AD. Christianity was then an illegal religion and was punished with death, torturing and confiscations. The public renunciation of Christ and the return to a religion recognized by the Roman State (such as paganism or even Judaism) was presented by the persecutors of the Christians as solution to the "problem". Especially for those with Jewish background as the Hebrew believers, who were the original recipients of the epistle, the return to the synagogue and to the familiar Judaism might have seemed appealing. However such a return demanded the public renunciation of Christ in front of the synagogue, thus putting Him in open shame[4]. Perhaps that's why the author takes special effort to warn his audience against something like this, making also clear the consequences.

Closing this strong warning we find the encouraging words of verse 9:

"Though we speak in this way, yet in your case, beloved, we feel sure of better things — things that belong to salvation."

---

they "were enlightened, and have tasted the heavenly gift, and have become partakers of the Holy Spirit, and have tasted the good word of God and the powers of the age to come".

[4] For more on the background of Hebrews see: David Pawson, Unlocking the Bible, Harper Collins Publishers, 2003, pp. 1115-1118 and Roger Hahn, The Book of Hebrews Lesson 1, found online here: http://www.crivoice.org/biblestudy/bbheb1.html

And with the words of John Wesley: "We are persuaded of you things that accompany salvation. We are persuaded you are now saved from your sins; and that you have that faith, love, and holiness, which lead to final salvation. Though we thus speak - to warn you, lest you should fall from your present steadfastness."

## 5.7. HEBREWS 10:23-29, 35-39: "IF WE SIN WILLFULLY", "IF ANYONE DRAWS BACK".

Continuing in Hebrews, we find one more strong warning in Hebrews 10. There we read:

Hebrews 10:23-29, 35-39
"Let us hold fast the confession of our hope without wavering, for he who promised is faithful. And let us consider how to stir up one another to love and good works, not neglecting to meet together, as is the habit of some, but encouraging one another, and all the more as you see the Day drawing near. *For if we sin willfully after we have received the knowledge of the truth, there no longer remains a sacrifice for sins, but a certain fearful expectation of judgment, and fiery indignation which will devour the adversaries.* Anyone who has rejected Moses' law dies without mercy on the testimony of two or three witnesses. Of how much worse punishment, do you suppose, will he be thought worthy who has trampled the Son of God underfoot, counted the blood of the covenant by which he was sanctified a common thing, and insulted the Spirit of grace? .... Therefore do not cast away your confidence, which has great reward. For you have need of endurance, so that after you have done the will of God, you may receive the promise: "For yet a little while, and He who is coming will come and will not tarry. Now the just shall live by faith; *but if anyone draws back, my soul has no pleasure in him.*" *But we are not of those who draw back and are destroyed but of those who believe to the saving of the soul.*"

Again three fundamental questions, whose answer is obvious from the text:

i) Does this passage and especially its strong warning refer to believers? The answer is yes it does: it speaks about people who have been sanctified with the blood of the covenant and no doubt such people can only be Christians. As 1 Corinthians 6:9-11 says, speaking to Christians:

"Or do you not know that the unrighteous will not inherit the kingdom of God? Do not be deceived: neither the sexually immoral, nor idolaters, nor adulterers, nor men who practice homosexuality, nor thieves, nor the greedy, nor drunkards, nor revilers, nor swindlers will inherit the kingdom of God. And such were some of you. *But you were washed, you were sanctified, you were justified in the name of the Lord Jesus Christ and by the Spirit of our God.* "

Sanctification and forgiveness of sins is something reserved for those who believe, and the means to obtain it is the "blood of the covenant" (Matthew 26:28).

ii) Now is it possible for someone who was sanctified with the blood of the covenant – the blood of Christ - to turn around and count this most precious blood as common, trampling the Son of God underfoot and insulting the holy spirit? Is it possible for someone who once believed to "draw back"? It is clear from this passage, and from the other passages we have looked at, that this is indeed possible.

iii) The next question is: is salvation what awaits those who though sanctified with the blood of the covenant they counted it as common insulting the spirit of grace? It is obvious from the text that the answer is negative.

Furthermore I want to point out the following part of the passage:

"For if we sin willfully after we have received the knowledge of the truth, there no longer remains a sacrifice for sins, but a certain fearful expectation of judgment, and fiery indignation which will devour the adversaries."

Later in the book we will speak more about sinning and when someone is really out of the faith. But whoever wants a short answer now, this perhaps is in the "sinning willfully after we have received the knowledge of the truth". "Sinning willfully" does not mean to sin once, having an episode of sin in a life that otherwise strives to practice righteousness. Instead, what is meant is a life that *practices* sin, a life that *habitually*, and as a way of life sins, despite the knowledge of the truth. This willful and habitual disregard of whatever we know God's Word says is deadly and the respective person should immediately repent instead of resting in a false sense of security concerning his salvation.

## 5.8. EXPLAINING AWAY HEBREWS 6 AND HEBREWS 10

Many of those who cherish the belief that the moment somebody believes he is saved once and for all and regardless of what will happen to his faith after that, seeing that Hebrews 6 and Hebrews 10 do not line up with this belief, have tried to find ways to explain these passages. Most of these explanations basically support that these do not refer believers. But if a person who has been sanctified by the blood of Jesus and has been a partaker of the holy spirit was never a believer, then who is a believer?

Others though, despite that they still support this doctrine, they cannot deny the obvious taught in these passages that they indeed refer to believers. One of them is Barnes, a well-known commentator, whose commentaries one can find in many online Bible programs. He said the following in his comments on Hebrews 10:26:

"If after we are converted and become true Christians we should apostatize, it would be impossible to be recovered again, for there would be no other sacrifice for sin; no way by which we could be saved. This passage, however, like Hebrews 6:4-6, has given rise to much difference of opinion. But that the above is the correct interpretation, seems evident to me from the following considerations:

(1) It is the natural and obvious interpretation, such as would occur probably to ninety-nine readers in a hundred, if there were no theory to support, and no fear that it would conflict with some other doctrine.

(2) it accords with the scope of the Epistle, which is, to keep those whom the apostle addressed from returning again to the Jewish religion, under the trials to which they were subjected.

(3) it is in accordance with the fair meaning of the language - the words "after that we have received the knowledge of the truth," referring more naturally to true conversion than to any other state of mind.

(4) the sentiment would not be correct if it referred to any but real Christians. It would not be true that one who had been somewhat enlightened, and who then sinned "willfully," must look on fearfully to the judgment without a possibility of being saved. There are multitudes of cases where such persons are saved. They "willfully" resist the Holy Spirit; they strive against him; they for a long time refuse to yield, but they are brought again to reflection, and are led to give their hearts to God.

(5) it is true, and always will be true, that if a sincere Christian should apostatize he could never be converted again; see the notes on Heb. 6:4-6. The reasons are obvious. He would have tried the only plan of salvation, and it would have failed. He would have embraced the Savior, and there would not have been efficacy enough in his blood to keep him, and there would be no more powerful Savior and no more efficacious blood of atonement. He would have renounced the Holy Spirit, and would have shown that his influences were not effectual to keep him, and there would be no other agent of greater power to renew and save him after he had apostatized. For these reasons it seems clear to me

that this passage refers to true Christians, and that the doctrine here taught is, that if such an one should apostatize, he must look forward only to the terrors of the judgment, and to final condemnation."

Therefore, according to Barnes these passages could only refer to real Christians. However, he chose to explain the above facts away. How? Through the following theory:

"If then it should be asked whether I believe that any true Christian ever did, or ever will fall from grace, and wholly lose his religion, I would answer unhesitatingly, no! If then it be asked what was the use of a warning like this, I answer: it would show the great sin of apostasy from God *if it were to occur*. It is proper to state the greatness of an act of sin, *though it might never occur*, in order to show how it would be regarded by God." (emphasis added).

In other words, according to Barnes, God is basically kidding us! He tells us what a great destruction one would suffer if he would abandon the faith, though such thing is, supposedly, impossible. He devotes passage upon passage with the sole purpose of warning us of something that – according to Barnes - is not really a danger! Would our God ever do something like this? No, He would not. God does not play with us. Let us be assured: what He says, *He also means it!*

From our side now, we can choose a bizarre explanation to avoid Hebrews 6 and 10 or we can just choose to believe what we read not just in Hebrews but also in the other passages covered in this study.

## 5.9. HEBREWS 3:4-6: HOLDING FAST OUR CONFIDENCE UNTIL THE END

Further in Hebrews, in chapter 3 we read:
Hebrews 3:4-6
"For every house is built by someone, but the builder of all things is God. Now Moses was faithful in all His house as a servant, for a testimony of those things which were to be spoken later; but Christ was faithful as a Son over His house — *whose house we are, if we hold fast our confidence and the boast of our hope firm until the end.*"

And the passage continues:

Hebrews 3:7-14
"Therefore, as the Holy Spirit says, "Today, if you hear his voice, do not harden your hearts as in the rebellion, on the day of testing in the wilderness, where your fathers put me to the test and saw my works for forty years. Therefore I was provoked with that generation, and said, 'They always go astray in their heart; they have not known my ways.' As I swore in my wrath, 'They shall not enter my rest.' *Take care, brothers, lest there be in any of you an evil, unbelieving heart, leading you to fall away from the living God.* But exhort one another every day, as long as it is called "today," that none of you may be hardened by the deceitfulness of sin. *For we have come to share in Christ, if indeed we hold our original confidence firm to the end.*"

Is it possible for a Christian "to fall away from the living God"? "Take care *brothers*" is how the related passage starts. Therefore, yes it is possible for a brother to fall away from the living God.

Furthermore, see also the two conditional statements starting with an "if". We are the house of Christ "*if* we hold fast our confidence and the boast of our hope firm *until the end*". And again "*we have come to share in Christ, if indeed we hold our original confidence firm to the end.*" Here we see once more what we have seen several times up to now: faith is a race with a beginning and an end. When is the end? If Christ has not come back during our lifetime, then the end is the end of our life. Else, it will be the time of His coming and our gathering to Him. Those who "hold their original confidence firm to the end", i.e. the ones who kept the faith *to the end* will enter the kingdom of God. But those who gave up the faith will not be there. They will NOT "share in Christ", nor will they be His house. This is what the "if" statements in these passages clearly say.

## 5.10. MATTHEW 24:13: "BUT THE ONE WHO ENDURES TO THE END WILL BE SAVED"

Along the same lines, and to return back for a moment to the gospel of Matthew, the Lord Jesus said:

Matthew 24:9-13
"Then they will deliver you up to tribulation and put you to death, and you will be hated by all nations for my name's sake. And then many will fall away and betray one another and hate one another. And many false prophets will arise and lead many astray. And because lawlessness will be increased, the love of many will grow cold. *But the one who endures to the end will be saved.*"

Some may say that the Lord speaks here about the last days. And they will be right. But aren't now the last days? And to avoid opening an eschatological discussion here, which in any case is not really the subject of this study, even if these days were not part of the last days, would this make his last statement less valid today? As He said: "the one who *endures to the end* will be saved". Exactly the same we saw previously in Hebrews: "For we have come to share in Christ, *if* indeed we hold our original confidence *firm to the end*" (Hebrews 3:14). Faith is a race and to run it we need *endurance*. Those who endure not a little, not till the middle, but to the end, will be saved. The others, the ones who fell away and who did not endure will not be there. That is why the writer of Hebrews encourages us:

Hebrews 10:35-39
"Therefore do not throw away your confidence, which has a great reward. For *you have need of endurance, so that when you have done the will of God you may receive what is promised.* For, "Yet a little while, and the coming one will come and will not delay; but my righteous one shall live by faith, and if he shrinks back, my soul has no pleasure in him." *But we are not of those who shrink back and are destroyed, but of those who have faith* and preserve their souls."

We have need of *endurance,* so that after we have done the will of God we may receive what is promised. And as 1 John 2:25 tells us:

"And this is the *promise* that he made to us — *eternal life."*

Eternal life is a promise, the chief promise, but to receive it we need to endure to the end. Those who abandoned the race, those who did not endure but shrank back will not receive the promise. And the writer of the Hebrews encourages us again:

Hebrews 12:1-2
"Therefore, since we are surrounded by so great a cloud of witnesses, let us also lay aside every weight, and sin which clings so closely, and *let us run with endurance the race that is set before us, looking to Jesus, the founder and perfecter of our faith,* who for the joy that was set before him endured the cross, despising the shame, and is seated at the right hand of the throne of God."

We have a race to run and there is only one way to run it: with endurance and looking unto Jesus, the founder and perfecter of our faith. And running with endurance, having our eyes fixed on Jesus and on what is promised to us, we will bear the fruit which marks the true disciples of Christ, the fruit the people of the fourth category of the parable of the sower bore:

"As for that in the good soil, they are those who, hearing the word, hold it fast in an honest and good heart, and *bear fruit with patience*."

The word "patience" is exactly the same Greek word translated as "endurance" in Hebrews 10:36 and 12:1. The ones in the fourth category are those who endure, who keep on running having their eyes on the Lord and with patience, as they abide in the vine, in Christ, they bear fruit. May all of us be in that category and remain in that category and if any of us is not in it may he repent and "run with endurance the race that is set before us".

## 5.11. 1 JOHN 2:24-25 – "IF WHAT YOU HEARD FROM THE BEGINNING ABIDES IN YOU"

Leaving Hebrews, let's now go to 1 John 2:24-25. There we read:

"Let what you heard from the beginning abide in you. *If* what you heard from the beginning abides in you, then you too will abide in the Son and in the Father. And this is the promise that he made to us – eternal life."

Whom is John addressing here? This is clear from verse 21 where he said to his audience: "I write to you, not because you do not know the truth, but because you know it, and because no lie is of the truth". So his audience is believers, people who know the truth. Now to these believers John said that if what they had heard from the beginning i.e. the Word of God, abided in them, they too would abide in the Son and in the Father. By this it is obvious that it is possible that somebody who has heard and knows the truth – as these ones here knew the truth (verse 21) - ceases to abide (to stay) in the truth. This is what this "if" in the passage means ("*If* what you heard from the beginning abides in you"). As John makes clear only those in whose heart the Word of God continues to abide, to live, abide in the Son and in the Father.

In other words and reading it differently: if the Word of God has ceased to abide in the heart of someone then he too has ceased to abide, to be in the Son and in the Father. And what happens in a case like this? John clarifies it a few verses later, in verse 28:

1 John 2:28
"And now, little children, abide in him, *so that* when he appears *we may have confidence and not shrink from him in shame at his coming.*"

See this "so that". When we see a "so that" we know that what follows it is completely dependent on what precedes it. There is only one way we will not be ashamed and shrink from Him in shame at His coming: this is by *abiding in Him*. And to abide in Him, we read it in 1 John 1:24-25, we have to have His Word abiding, living in us. Only then we abide in Him. To avoid confusion, let us summarize:

i) we will not be ashamed at his coming, if we abide in Him (1 John 2:28).

ii) And abiding in Him means that His Word abides, lives, in us (1 John 2:24-25)

Therefore, abiding in the Lord is not something we did once and then we abide in Him forever and ever, regardless of how we live, regardless of whether the Word of God lives really in us. If it was like this there would be no reason for John, speaking to believers to encourage them to have the Word abiding in them and to abide in Christ. On the contrary, abiding in Him is a decision which although we took once it also has to be our decision today.

The phrase "abide in Him" is John's way of telling us "fight the good fight of faith", "continue in the faith", "continue in His kindness", "run the race that is set before you", and the other phrases we saw Paul and the author of the Hebrews using. It is his way of telling us the same thing. And reading 1 John 2:28 in a different way: since we need to abide in Him so that we will not be ashamed at His coming, then it is clear that those that will not abide in Him will be ashamed at His coming. This then gives us a hint of how we are to understand passages like Romans 9:33:

"As it is written, Behold, I lay in Zion a stumbling stone and rock of offence: *and whosoever believes on him shall not be ashamed.*"

Note that in this passage the present tense is used ("whosoever believes"), declaring that the faith it speaks about is a *present* reality. Unfortunately some overlook this and read it as if it was speaking for something that happened once in the past, i.e. as follows: "whoever, once upon a time, believed in Him regardless of what he later did concerning his faith shall not be ashamed". But the truth is different, as according to John, we will not be ashamed at His coming if we not only start in Him but also ABIDE (i.e. stay) in Him. The "whosoever believes in Him shall not be ashamed" of Romans 9:33 refers then to people who "believe" ( now in the present) and will be found abiding in Him at his coming, or the end of their life found them abiding in Him. These will not be ashamed. However, those who His coming will find them not abiding in Him will be ashamed.  In fact the Lord made this even clearer when He gave the parable of the vine:

John 15:5-6
"I am the vine; you are the branches. *Whoever abides in me* and I in him, he it is that bears much fruit, for apart from me you can do nothing. *If anyone does not abide in me* he is thrown away like a branch and withers; and the branches are gathered, thrown into the fire, and burned."

Again, some who have been taught that the grace of God means that it is enough for salvation that somebody just starts in the faith may feel uncomfortable with the above. As it is clear from the above passages it is not enough that somebody only starts in the faith but he also needs to finish in what he started. He needs to abide in the Lord and His Word to abide in Him. Else, if he does not abide, "he is thrown away like a branch and withers; and the branches are gathered, thrown into the fire, and burned". Some may think that it is without compassion, impolite and unloving to speak about such possibilities. Unfortunately many times in our age we consider it loving to consistently hide the truth so that we do not make some feel uncomfortable. But the hiding of the truth is a lie and in no way constitutes love. Let us not succumb to what is nothing more than the spirit of this age. If the Word of God, if the God who never lies and Who is the Love itself, tells us such things, then the best I think we need to do it to take them seriously into consideration.

## 5.12. 2 JOHN 8-9 : TO "EVERYONE WHO GOES ON AHEAD AND DOES NOT ABIDE IN THE TEACHING OF CHRIST

Moving on to the second epistle of John, in verses 8 and 9 we read:

"Watch yourselves, so that you may not lose what we have worked for, but may win a full reward. *Everyone who goes on ahead and does not abide in the teaching of Christ, does not have God. Whoever abides in the teaching has both the Father and the Son.*"

Again John uses the "abiding" as a measure. Abiding means staying. To abide in something you need, after you have started it, to make up your mind to continue in it, to stay in it. To have the Father and the Son, to have them coming and making their home with us, we have to abide in the teaching of Christ i.e. to abide in His Word. Indeed as the Lord said:

John 14:23-24
"Jesus answered him, "*If* anyone loves me, he will keep my word, *and* my Father will love him, *and* we will come to him *and* make our home with him. Whoever does not love me does not keep my

74

words. And the word that you hear is not mine but the Father's who sent me."

Again there is an "if" and there is an "and" (in fact three of them). *If* we love Christ then we will keep His Word, we will abide in His teaching. *And,* as a result, the Father will love us and He with His Son will come and make their home in us. But if we do not keep His Word, if we do not abide in the teaching of Christ, then this means that we do not love Him, and in turn it means that we have neither the Father nor the Son. Many may not like these words, but they are the plain truth of the Word of God.

## 5.13. 2 PETER 1:5-11 : "MAKE EVERY EFFORT TO SUPPLEMENT YOUR FAITH"

Moving now to 2 Peter 1:5-11 we read:

2 Peter 1:5-7
"For this very reason, *make every effort to supplement your faith* with virtue, and virtue with knowledge, and knowledge with self-control, and self-control with steadfastness, and steadfastness with godliness, and godliness with brotherly affection, and brotherly affection with love."

Does our faith need to be supplemented? According to Peter yes it does. With what does it need to be supplemented? Here it is: virtue, knowledge, self-control, steadfastness, godliness, brotherly affection, love. See that Peter does not say: "if you want, here is a nice-to-have list". In contrast, what he says is very emphatic: "*make every effort*". Being in the faith then does involve effort, effort to add to our faith those things which Peter says. And who makes this effort? Very simply: *We.* Yes with the help of the Lord, but this help is not coercion but a working together with us (see also 1 Corinthians 3:6-9).

What Peter says, Paul also tells us, with different wording, in Galatians 5:22-26:

Galatians 5:22-26
"But the fruit of the Spirit [the new nature, the new man] is love, joy, peace, patience, kindness, goodness, faithfulness, gentleness, self-control; against such things there is no law. And those who belong to Christ Jesus have crucified the flesh with its passions and desires. *If we live by the Spirit, let us also keep in step with the Spirit.* Let us not become conceited, provoking one another, envying one another."

And Romans 12:1-2
"I appeal to you therefore, brothers, by the mercies of God, to present your bodies as a living sacrifice, holy and acceptable to God, which is your spiritual worship. *Do not be conformed to this world, but be transformed by the renewal of your mind,* that by testing you may discern what is the will of God, what is good and acceptable and perfect."

What both the apostles tell us is: "walk with the new man, not the old man; renew your mind; supplement your faith".

Back to 2 Peter: let's now assume that, though the Word says "make every effort to supplement your faith", somebody chooses not to supplement his faith and makes no effort in this direction. What will happen in this case? We may find the answer by looking at what happens when somebody does supplement his faith. This is given in verse 8 of 2 Peter 1:

"For *if* these qualities are yours and are increasing, *they keep you from being ineffective or unfruitful in the knowledge of our Lord Jesus Christ.*"

So if we "make every effort to supplement our faith" with these qualities then we will be neither ineffective nor unfruitful in the knowledge of our Lord. This in turn means that a person who

76

does not do this and makes no effort (not to say every effort) to supplement his faith will be both ineffective and unfruitful in the knowledge of our Lord Jesus Christ. And Peter continues:

2 Peter 1:9
"For whoever lacks these qualities is so nearsighted that he is blind, having forgotten that he was cleansed from his former sins."

Whoever makes no effort to supplement his faith and therefore lacks these qualities is called blind; a person who has forgotten that he was cleansed from his former sins, exactly like the person in the parable of the debtor of the 10000 talents who had forgotten the generosity of his master and from what He cleansed him. And Peter carries on:

2 Peter 1:10
"Therefore, brothers, rather *be diligent to make your calling and election sure*, for if you do these things, you shall never fall."

Why should we be diligent to make our calling and election sure if these were made sure in the past, once and for all, the moment we believed? Because that moment we *started* in the faith, but this faith has to also take roots; it has to be supplemented; it has to become fruitful. And Peter continues:

2 Peter 1:11
"*For so* an entrance shall be ministered unto you abundantly into the everlasting kingdom of our Lord and Savior Jesus Christ."

"For so" means "by these means", "in this way", "because of this" will an entrance into the everlasting kingdom of our Lord and Savior shall be ministered to us abundantly. Because of what? Because of what we read in the preceding verses: because of making every effort to supplement our faith with what Peter told us, which in turn means that we did not become ineffective and unfruitful but we were diligent to make our calling and election sure. By these means, for this reason, will be given to us an abundant entrance into the Kingdom of God.

Now the above brings to my mind the following thought and question: does it mean that those who were diligent to make their faith a fruitful faith, as the fourth category of the parable of the sower did, will get a very warm welcome into the Kingdom of God, but those who did not do this and who were or became fruitless will also get an entrance but a rather cool one? A look back to chapters 2 and 3 and to the sayings of the King shows who He will welcome. And from what I read my understanding is that only the ready ones will be welcomed. This does not mean that only faultless and sinless will get into the Kingdom. There is none like this, except the Lord Himself. What it means is that we are alerted, that we take care of our faith, trying to live it out. It is one thing though to try to live out our faith and fall here and there and quite another if someone lives out, practices, sin as a habit and way of life, ignoring whatever faith he had. Neither the 5 fool virgins, nor the unfruitful servant, nor the one that abandoned the vine will find the door of the Kingdom open. Let these be for us examples for avoidance.

Therefore, may we take care of our faith and despite our mistakes and failures may we supplement it "with virtue, and virtue with knowledge, and knowledge with self-control, and self-control with steadfastness, and steadfastness with godliness, and godliness with brotherly affection, and brotherly affection with love ..... For in this way there will be richly provided for us an entrance into the eternal kingdom of our Lord and Savior Jesus Christ."

### 5.14. PHILIPPIANS 2:12-16: "WORK OUT YOUR SALVATION WITH FEAR AND TREMBLING"

The next passage we will look at is Philippians 2:12-16. There we read:

Philippians 2:12-16

"Therefore, my beloved, as you have always obeyed, so now, not only as in my presence but much more in my absence, *work out your own salvation with fear and trembling*, for it is God who works in you, both to will and to work for his good pleasure. Do all things without grumbling or disputing, that you may be blameless and innocent, children of God without blemish in the midst of a crooked and twisted generation, among whom you shine as lights in the world, *holding fast to the word of life, so that in the day of Christ I may be proud that I did not run in vain or labor in vain.*"

To "work out our salvation", means to live out our faith, to walk like a follower, a disciple, of Christ. Now, is this optional? Is it a nice thing to do but never mind if it does not happen? Well the phrase "with fear and trembling" does not sound optional. This phrase means that we should take the working out, the practicing, of our faith, *very* seriously; so seriously to the point of fear and trembling. To use the words that we saw Peter using in the previous section: we should "make *every effort*".

Furthermore, Paul tells the Philippians to "hold fast to the word of life". If they did this, then in the day of Christ he would be proud that he did not run or labor in vain. This in turn means that if they did not hold fast to the Word, the labor of Paul would indeed be in vain. And the question is why? If these people, regardless of what happened to their faith after they believed, regardless of whether or not they held fast to the Word and abided in the vine, would be in the Kingdom of God, then the work of Paul would not be in vain, wasted. Correct? Some made it into the Kingdom and this is not vain at all. Personally the only reasonable explanation I have for this is that if the Philippians did not hold fast to the Word, abiding in the vine, then they would not be in the Kingdom and yes then Paul's labor would be in vain, like it never happened.

## 5.15. 1 TIMOTHY 6:10-16: THE LOVE OF MONEY

In 1 Timothy 6:10 we find a further example of people who wandered away from the faith: those who loved money.

1 Timothy 6:10
"For the love of money is a root of all kinds of evils. It is through this craving that *some have wandered away from the faith and pierced themselves with many pangs.*"

"Wandered away" is the Greek word "apeplanithisan" and it means "to be led astray, to be seduced". People who have wandered away, were once walking on the right path but then, because of a deception they followed through, they were led astray, they wandered away. As Paul says, the people he is speaking about here "wandered away *from the faith*", which consequently means that they were once in it.

The deceitfulness of riches will cause those deceived by it to wander away from the faith. Using the parable of the vine in John 15, this is equal to wandering away from the vine. In turn this will make them unfruitful – third category of the parable of the sower – as there is no way to bear fruit without abiding in the vine[5]. Finally, if there is no true repentance and return, the end will be removal from the vine and classification of these "branches" with what will be burned (John 15:2, 6).

Concerning the love of money, it is obvious that it is a lethal enemy to the faith; it is a faith killer of the first degree. God does provide material blessings for the covering of our needs, but wanting to become rich, wanting to be "blessed" with riches is not something we should do. Instead here is what we should do:

---

[5] In any case, the deceitfulness of riches is mentioned explicitly in the parable of the sower as a thorn and a cause of unfruitfulness.

Hebrews 13:5-6

*"Keep your life free from love of money, and be content with what you have,* for he has said, "I will never leave you nor forsake you." So we can confidently say, "The Lord is my helper; I will not fear; what can man do to me?"

Are we doing this? Are we content with what we have? Is our life free from the love of money or we are running after riches? Let us think and make any adjustments needed.

## 5.15.1. On God as a blessing machine. Is He really something like this?

To make a digression from what we saw in this section, it is surprising to me that, given the solemn warnings of the Scripture concerning the desire to become rich, this very desire is cultivated from the pulpits of some churches and quite frequently through so called Christian Media and preachers shown in them. So people are taught and told to give abundantly to the so and so ministry (many times this happens under the non-valid threat of the tithe – see also my book: "Tithing, giving and the New Testament") with the promise that if they do this then God is obliged to "bless" them financially. Thus God is seen as a blessing machine where from the one side one puts his money and his "believing" (by "believing" what is usually meant is positive confessions through which the person that makes them tries to persuade himself that what he is asking will happen) and from the other side God pours out, in exchange, His blessings, with health and wealth be among the chief of them. However as it is clear from the Scriptures, as well as from tradition, none of the apostles nor of course Christ were rich. In fact according to tradition, *all* apostles save John were assassinated because of their faith. Despite this fact the churches of the preachers of the prosperity gospel are filled with thousands.  And though I do not have numbers to support it, I am sure that they will go through a very big trial when they find out - and I believe they will find it out - that God, despite His mercy, patience and grace does *not* work like a blessing machine. You cannot put God in a box as essentially the preachers of the prosperity gospel present it. I wish this was a fiction story, but unfortunately it is not. It happens now and to many. I feel for all these people, for I was one of them, moved away by promises of people that my life would essentially be without problems and exactly as I wanted it. But at one point in my life I came to realize the hard way that I was deceived. I realized then that I had to submit to God instead of God submitting to me. Also I realized that in Acts 12, before the widely known and widely preached record of Peter being miraculously delivered from the prison, you have the record of the apostle James, the brother of John, killed by the sword. The one apostle was delivered while the other was not. At the end even the one who was delivered (Peter) died, after some years, a martyr's death, exactly like James did. Some also forget this. The idea some have in their mind, is that God will deliver them from every small difficulty so that they can go on living in their "blessings" forever and ever and die happily (by this they mean rich, healthy etc.) at an old age. Suffering for Christ has not even crossed their mind, for in their view God is there to deliver them out of *all* suffering. And yet the Bible says (and this is just a sample):

Romans 8:16-17
"The Spirit himself bears witness with our spirit that we are children of God, and if children, then heirs — heirs of God and fellow heirs with Christ, *provided we suffer with him in order that we may also be glorified with him.*"

2 Timothy 2:3
"Share in *suffering* as a good soldier of Christ Jesus"

2 Timothy 3:12
"Indeed, *all who desire to live a godly life in Christ Jesus will be persecuted*"

Acts 14:21-22
"And when they [Paul and Barnabas] had preached the gospel to that city, and had taught many, they returned again to Lystra, and to Iconium, and Antioch, confirming the souls of the disciples, and exhorting them to continue in the faith, and that *we must through much tribulation enter into the kingdom of God.*"

Many think that suffering is not relevant to them, for Christ has already suffered for them. They will declare with boldness the first part of Romans 8:16-17 i.e. that "we are children of God, and if children, then heirs — heirs of God and fellow heirs with Christ". But the passage does not stop there. It carries on with a "provided", with an "if", a condition for the above: "*provided* we suffer with him that we may also be glorified with him". Suffering for Christ's sake is a honor. What happened to James and to almost all the apostles (martyrdom) was a honor and not a mishappening. The apostles themselves saw suffering for Christ's sake as something to rejoice in:

Acts 5:40-41
"and when they had called in the apostles, they beat them and charged them not to speak in the name of Jesus, and let them go. Then they left the presence of the council, *rejoicing that they were counted worthy to suffer dishonor for the name.*"

In the light of the above, I would like to ask us a question. Tacitus was a Roman historian and eyewitness to the first state-run persecution started by Nero (64-67 AD). He wrote about the events:

"In their very deaths they [he means the arrested Christians] were made the subjects of sport: for they were covered with the hides of wild beasts, and worried to death by dogs, or nailed to crosses, or set fire to, and when the day waned, burned to serve for the evening lights. Nero offered his gardens for this spectacle" (Chronicles, Book XV, para. 44).

Christians were put on fire as evening lights in Nero's garden! Can we really picture this? My question now: what would we do if a soldier came to our house to take us away from our family and "blessings" and put us on fire, unless we denied the Lord? Would we go? Or would we deny the Lord and the faith to save our blessings, because we perhaps believe that this Lord, since He is so much of love, would just choose to close His eyes? What would we do if God did not grant the most precious desire we have (spouse, kids, job, health etc.)? I do not say that He will not. I speak hypothetically. Would we still follow Him with no conditions attached? Let each one of us answer for himself.

## 5.15.2. On false teachers

Forgive me for continuing in this digression, but here it is perhaps a good opportunity to give some more information concerning false teachers. Peter spoke about them in 2 Peter 2:

2 Peter 2:1-3
"But false prophets also arose among the people, just as there will be *false teachers* among you, who will secretly bring in destructive heresies, even denying the Master who bought them, bringing upon themselves swift destruction. And *many* will follow their sensuality, and because of them *the way of truth will be blasphemed. And through covetousness shall they with feigned words make merchandise of you*: Their condemnation from long ago is not idle, and their destruction is not asleep." (ESV-KJV)

"*Many* will follow their sensuality": false teachers have apparently a large following. They are popular. Contrast this with the narrow gate that leads to life. It is not many who find it but *few*. The many go through the broad gate.

Matthew 7:13-14
"Enter by the narrow gate. For the gate is wide and the way is easy that leads to destruction, and those who enter by it are *many*. For the gate is narrow and the way is hard that leads to life, and those who find it are *few*."

The fact that somebody is a popular preacher does not necessarily mean that he is also a true teacher. It may well be that he is a false teacher and in fact his popularity is just because of this: because he gives the people an entrance through the broad gate and the easy way and many like this entrance and thus follow him.

Furthermore as Peter tells us: "and because of them *the way of truth* will be blasphemed". There is only one way of truth and this is the "hard way that leads to life". It is the way through the narrow gate. This way, the true and genuine Christianity, will be blasphemed. It will be perhaps branded as "religion", "legalism" etc. as opposed to the "freedom" and the "grace" (but cheap, falsified grace and not the grace of the Word) these false teachers promise. Also, the world, seeing these impostors and thinking that they are what they pretend to be ("Christians"), will come to wrong conclusions about Christianity as a whole, again causing the way of truth to be blasphemed. And Peter continues:

2 Peter 2:18-19
"For, speaking loud boasts of folly, they entice by sensual passions of the flesh those who are barely escaping from those who live in error. *They promise them freedom*, but they themselves are slaves of corruption."

"Freedom" is the main promise they sell but their promises are lies, for they themselves are slaves of corruption. And why do they do this? What is their motive? Again Peter gives us the answer:

2 Peter 2:3
"And through *covetousness* shall they with feigned words *make merchandise of you*"

I took this part from the KJV. The old translations use the above rendering, which corresponds exactly to what the Greek text says. The newer versions have the part "they with feigned words make merchandise of you" as "they will exploit you with false words", rendering the Greek verb "emporeuomai" as "to exploit". However this verb does not mean to exploit but "to trade, buy and sell, make merchandise" (Strong's dictionary). In other words, a characteristic of a false teacher is that he is greedy and in his greed he makes merchandise of the people of God. I do not know about you but to me this speaks volumes. Do you see "preachers" amassing huge property (including but not restricted to super luxury homes, jets, luxury cars, huge salaries etc.) all through "preaching"? I would say: run away! You do not need to hear anything else. This is the fruit of a greedy, false teacher who has merchandised the people of God, extorting "offerings" from them[6], selling them bogus books (many of them written by ghost writers), conferences and "advice" for big fees. "By the fruit you will know them" the Lord said and greed is a definite fruit of a false teacher that one can ignore only at his peril.

Now the greedy, false teacher "who perverts the grace of our God into a license for immorality and deny our only Master and Lord, Jesus Christ" (Jude 1:4) is not the only kind of false teacher. There is another one, in the other extreme and this is the kind which had plagued the churches in Galatia and was active in other churches too. Their teaching? That Christians should keep the law of Moses (see the book of Galatians), that they should abstain from foods (Hebrews 13:9), that they should not marry (1 Timothy 4:1-4), that they should "observe days, months and seasons" (Galatians 4:10), that they should worship angels

---

[6] Usually under the threat of tithing and the supposed horrible things that will happen to the followers if they do not give their tithe to the "ministry" (more accurate would be "business") of the preacher.

(Colossians 2:18) instead of God only, through the Lord Jesus Christ, that they should call to other mediators instead of the only "one mediator between God and men, the man Christ Jesus" (1 Timothy 2:5) etc. Those who were preaching or preach such things are false teachers too doing the same thing, as those on the other side: leading people astray, from the true Word of God, this time through false "humility" and "intruding into those things which they have not seen, vainly puffed up by their fleshly mind" (Colossians 2:18 – KJV).

Therefore, false teachers appear basically as two extremes: the one extreme is a perversion of the grace of God, turning it into a license for immorality, while the other is legalism, and following - through a cover up of false humility - after practices that God never intended. We need to beware of both.

To close this section, I would like to add the following clarification: though a false teacher messes up God's Word, mishandling it for selfish purposes, this does not mean that a Christian who makes a mistake in teaching God's Word is by definition a false teacher. As James says:

James 3:1-2a
"Not many of you should become teachers, my brothers, for you know that we who teach will be judged with greater strictness. *For we all stumble in many ways.*"

"We *all* stumble in many ways", says James, referring to teachers and very graciously including himself also. Making a mistake in teaching the Word of God does not necessarily make somebody a false teacher. Else we would all be false teachers, for according to James we all stumble in many ways. The truth is that we all learn and as we learn more, we may have to go back and teach more accurately what we had taught in the past. I am thankful to God that He does not wait until we reach perfection before He can use us! A false teacher is not somebody who, despite his sincerity and respect for the Word of God, makes a mistake in teaching it. The mistake of the false teacher is not "just a mistake". It is something much bigger. There is indeed a huge difference between making "just a mistake" and "perverting the grace of God into a license for immorality" (Jude 4) or "speaking twisted things to draw away the disciples after them" (Acts 20:30) or "through covetousness make with feigned words merchandise of the people of God" (2 Peter 2:3). The former, the one who makes "just a mistake" is not a false teacher, but a disciple that needs to fix his message (example here: Apollos in Acts 18: he did not have a 100% correct message but he got it fixed). The latter though, is indeed a false teacher, a wolf in sheep's clothing, an exploiter of the people of God who leads them astray and after himself. And though it is easy to imagine these exploiters as complete outsiders to the faith, this is not always so. Some of them are people who though they had started in the Lord they apostatized from Him afterwards. 2 Peter 2 devotes a large part to them. I have left the related passages, as well as the similar ones from Jude, for the end of this chapter. For the time being let us go to Galatians.

## 5.16. GALATIANS 5:2-4 "SEVERED FROM CHRIST"

In the epistle to the Galatians Paul deals with the matter of law and grace and the fact that we are saved by grace, by God's unmerited favor, without the works of the law. The reason he was saying this was because some were teaching the Galatians that they had to keep the law and that they even had to be circumcised. As we said previously, there are, broadly speaking, two versions of false teachers: the one leads people astray by effectively perverting the grace of God into a license for immorality (Jude 1:4) and the other leads them astray through legalism i.e. through imposing adherence to the law of Moses (Sabbath, circumcision, tithe, ceremonies etc.) and to things that God never intended for believers. The Galatians had fallen victims of this second type of false teachers. Paul dealt with the issue making clear what such departure from the true Gospel would mean:

Galatians 5:2-4
"Look: I, Paul, say to you that if you accept circumcision, Christ will be of no advantage to you. I testify again to every man who accepts circumcision that he is obligated to keep the whole law. *You are severed from Christ, you who would be justified by the law; you have fallen away from grace.*"

You cannot be severed from something, if you were never one with it. These people were true believers, one with Christ. However, this would change if they sought justification through the law. In that case they would be severed from Christ and they would fall away from grace. Therefore it is indeed possible to be severed from Christ and fall away from grace i.e. to be with Him today but to no longer be with Him in the future, to have ourselves severed from Him, by - in the case of Galatians - following a perverted doctrine. Notice also that *they* would fall away from grace. It is not that grace would expel them but rather that *they* themselves would fall away from it. *Therefore grace holds us as long as we want to be held by it. But if one wants it, he could fall away from it.*

Furthermore, as Paul testifies of them just a couple of verses later:

Galatians 5:7
"You *were* running well. Who hindered you from obeying the truth?"

See that he uses past tense: they *were* running well. But no longer. Somebody hindered them, obviously by teaching them to obey the law and get circumcised. As a result, they were no longer running well. Instead, they were on their way to be led astray. Therefore, it is possible to run well but then to stop running well and even be led astray i.e. fall away from the right path and out of the race of faith altogether.

Now the question to be asked is: if somebody is severed from Christ and therefore he falls away from grace, will He still be saved? I believe the answer is clear in Ephesians 2:8 and in John 15. According to Ephesians salvation is *by grace through faith*. If these Galatians would fall away from grace then they would no longer fall into the case of Ephesians 2:8. In addition, according to John 15:6 :

"If anyone does not abide in me he is thrown away like a branch and withers; and the branches are gathered, thrown into the fire, and burned."

Whoever does not abide in Christ, whoever is severed from Him, has the end described in the above passage and which in turn also tells us what would happen in the case of the Galatians that would be severed from Christ.

To summarize: yes, is it possible that a believer is, because of following a deception, severed from Christ. And this, as in the case of Galatians, can happen when someone replaces the work of Christ with the law and tries to attain righteousness through it.

Unfortunately some misuse Galatians to go to the other extreme, saying that God cares only for our faith and the works have no real importance, as if faith and works could exist separately from each other. But it is not really like this. As Luther very correctly said:

*"it is impossible to separate faith and works as it is to separate heat and light from fire[7]"*.

---

[7] Luther: An introduction to St. Paul's letter to the Romans.

This is true. There is no salvation but only by faith and there is no true faith without the respective fruit, the works that should normally accompany it. Fruitless "faith" cannot save, not because the fruit would supposedly save us and this is missing. In contrast, it cannot save us because fruitless faith is not a true faith. It is dead as James said (James 2:26) and such faith does not save. The message of this book is in no way salvation through works. There is NO such salvation! What there is is salvation through faith, a faith though that has to be kept to the end and which should be  - and will be if we stay united with Christ – fruitful. In fact I would summarize the message of this book in the passage from Galatians 5:6 we saw earlier:

"in Christ Jesus neither circumcision nor uncircumcision counts for anything, but only *faith working through love.*"

Faith, love, works (action)! All three go together and I do not think that any of these can really exist as stand-alone and without the others.

## 5.17. 2 TIMOTHY 2:11-13: "IF WE DENY HIM, HE WILL ALSO DENY US"

The next passage we will check is 2 Timothy 2:11-13. There we read:

2 Timothy 2:11-13
"The saying is trustworthy, for: If we have died with him, we will also live with him; if we endure, we will also reign with him; *if we deny him, he also will deny us;* if we are faithless, he remains faithful— for he cannot deny himself."

The word "him", obviously refers to Christ as He is the one who has died and will reign. Now can we deny Christ? Again, if there was no such possibility then Paul would have never mentioned it. Yes then, it is possible that somebody denies Him. He should NOT deny Him, but deceived he may end up doing it. What will happen in this case? The Word leaves no space for speculation: *"if we deny him, he will also deny us"*.

To avoid these plain words many go to verse 33 and say: "but see verse 33: "if we are faithless, he remains faithful — for he cannot deny himself". Then they try to use this verse to support that if we deny Him is actually nothing that serious for He is faithful and He will not actually deny us. But such an interpretation is obviously wrong, for just one verse before we read it plainly and clearly: if we deny Him, He will deny us. What verse 33 actually tells us is that He is always faithful, but this does not mean that He accepts us even when we deny Him, because one verse earlier Paul settled this question. It is a contrast between us, if we are faithless, and Him, who is always faithful. Christ is never going to be faithless! We may choose to be faithless but He is never that way. He is always faithful.

## 5.18. JAMES 5:19-20: THE WANDERED BROTHER

Reading further, let us go to James 5:19-20:

"My brothers, *if anyone among you wanders from the truth* and someone brings him back, let him know that whoever brings back a sinner from his wandering *will save his soul from death* and will cover a multitude of sins."

The phrase "If anyone among you wanders from the truth", makes clear that a brother – and this text refers to brothers: "My brothers, if *anyone among you.."* – can wander from the truth. What does this mean? He can err in teaching and be led astray – as those Galatians who wanted to follow the law as means of getting justified – or follow after sinful practices. Concerning the latter, we are not speaking here about a sin while we are walking on the right way (see later our discussion on 1 John). Rather we are speaking of somebody who wanders from the truth, wanders from the light and walks now in darkness. So, is it possible that "anyone among us" wanders from the truth? Unfortunately, yes it is.

Now James says that if a brother brings back somebody who wanders from the truth he "will save his soul *from death*". The passage, speaking about death of that soul, makes clear that if the respective person does not return he will not at the end receive eternal life but the exact opposite of it. And this despite the fact that he was once on the right path. The same truth we find also in other places in the epistles. Here are some:

Romans 8:13
"For if you live according to the flesh you will die, but if by the Spirit you put to death the deeds of the body, you will live."

Galatians 6:7-8
"Do not be deceived: God is not mocked, for whatever one sows, that will he also reap. For the one who sows to his own flesh will from the flesh reap corruption, but the one who sows to the Spirit will from the Spirit reap eternal life."

Hebrews 10:26-27
"For if we sin willfully after we have received the knowledge of the truth, there no longer remains a sacrifice for sins, but a certain fearful expectation of judgment, and fiery indignation which will devour the adversaries."

We reap eternal life when we run the race of faith, sowing to the Spirit and to the new nature. Paul is very clear: "the one who sows to the Spirit will from the Spirit *reap eternal life.*" This does not mean that we are faultless or sinless. Nobody is. These however are mistakes *while on the way.* We strive to live a life of righteousness and sometimes we may have some episodes of sin here and there. But they are just that: episodes, not something we are really practicing, living as a way of life. If however, we essentially live a life of sin, we work lawlessness, we live - habitually and as a way of life - according to the flesh, then we will reap what we sowed and from what we read this is "a fearful expectation of judgment, and a fury of fire", corruption and death. Now some may ask: "but why? Is it not salvation by faith?" Yes it is, but true faith and living according to the flesh never go together. They are mutually exclusive. We cannot be in both at the same time.

## 5.19. "SOME WILL ABANDON THE FAITH"

Moving on in 1 Timothy 4 we read:

1 Timothy 4:1-3
"The Spirit clearly says that in later times *some will abandon the faith* and follow deceiving spirits and things taught by demons. Such teachings come through hypocritical liars, whose consciences have been seared as with a hot iron. They forbid people to marry and order them to abstain from certain foods, which God created to be received with thanksgiving by those who believe and who know the truth."

If somebody who came to the faith could *never* abandon it then it would also be impossible for these people the Spirit is speaking about here to do that. But as it is obvious this is not impossible. How does it happen in their case? By falling victim to false teachers, who in turn are but instruments of deceiving spirits. We spoke previously about two main groups of false teachers. It seems to me that the false teachers of the above passage belong to the second group, the legalistic one, which uses false humility and promotes that a person can supposedly come to God through such things as abstinence from food or denying marriage. This is again so relevant. In fact it was only a few hundred years after Paul wrote the above, in the council of Elvira in 306 AD when, according to Canon 33: "all bishops, presbyters, and deacons and all other clerics were to abstain completely from their wives and not to have children" thus opening the way to the obligation of celibacy, which later became a requirement for ministers of some denominations.

False teachers will always lead people astray and we need to watch out. It is nevertheless impossible to watch out if we do not know *for ourselves* what the Word of God says. Are we reading the Word of God on our own, without the "glasses" of cherished doctrines, or do we essentially base our faith on what others say about the Word? There are many cherished beliefs that people have, yet sad to say: *they would not arrive to them by reading the Bible on their own, without somebody teaching them these beliefs.* They only "see" these "truths", if they put on the particular "glasses" of interpreting Scripture that somebody has given them. But the Scripture interprets itself and needs no such glasses.

Closing this section I exhort us: let us pick up our Bible and read it thoroughly, focusing on what the text says and without filtering the text through theories and theological doctrines we may have heard. God says what He means and He means what He says. If a particular doctrine is in the Bible, you will clearly see it when you read it. But if a doctrine can only be "seen", after you put on particular "glasses" of interpreting the Scriptures, I would be very careful in considering this doctrine as Biblical.

### 5.20. 1 TIMOTHY 5:8: "HE HAS DENIED THE FAITH AND IS WORSE THAN AN UNBELIEVER"

To see an example of how Paul meant faith and that for him it was not just a confession but a way of living, let's go to 1 Timothy 5. There  Paul is writing to Timothy about the widows and the obligations that children and grandchildren have to them. Verses 3 and 4 tell us:

1 Timothy 5:3-4

"Honor widows who are truly widows. But if a widow has children or grandchildren, let them first learn to show godliness to their own household and to make some return to their parents, for this is pleasing in the sight of God."

God cares for the widows and He commanded that first children and grandchildren take care of their needs. This is the declared will of God. Now let's suppose that a believer with widows in his family, denies to do this. Paul speaks about this case in no unclear terms in 1 Timothy 5:8:

"But if anyone does not provide for his relatives, and especially for members of his household, *he has denied the faith and is worse than an unbeliever.*"

I do not think anybody would speak like this today. People today are afraid of speaking the truth, lest they offend somebody. But Paul did not have such problems and I am sure he loved the people probably more than all of us. In fact I believe he did not have such concerns exactly because he loved them. Paul and the other apostles and first and foremost the Lord Himself, never considered faith as something that cannot be denied, nor did they consider someone faithful just because he said so. When Paul said to the Corinthians to examine themselves whether they were in the faith, he was not referring to people who had verbally denied the Lord. These were definitely *not* in the faith. Instead he was referring to believers, to people who thought that they were in the faith and yet perhaps denied to practice it, denying for example to take care of the members of their household, including their widowed mother or grandmother. Such ones were not in the faith and though they had never verbally denied the Lord, they did so practically, by their acts. Therefore, denying the faith does not mean I stand up and make a confession with my mouth against the faith (though this can happen too). More frequently it means *I deny to practice it*, to do - consistently and habitually - what accompanies the faith, living it out. Paul, using the case of a so

96

called believer who denied taking care of his household, said that he had denied the faith and he was worse than an unbeliever.

## 5.21. "GO AND SIN NO MORE": WHAT THE LORD EXPECTS FROM FORGIVEN SINNERS.

In John 8:3-11 we have an indicative record of the Lord's great love, compassion and forgiveness for sinners. Let's read it:

John 8:3-11
"The scribes and the Pharisees brought a woman who had been caught in adultery, and placing her in the midst they said to him, "Teacher, this woman has been caught in the act of adultery. Now in the Law Moses commanded us to stone such women. So what do you say?" This they said to test him, that they might have some charge to bring against him. Jesus bent down and wrote with his finger on the ground. And as they continued to ask him, he stood up and said to them, "Let him who is without sin among you be the first to throw a stone at her." And once more he bent down and wrote on the ground. But when they heard it, they went away one by one, beginning with the older ones, and Jesus was left alone with the woman standing before him. Jesus stood up and said to her, "Woman, where are they? Has no one condemned you?" She said, "No one, Lord." And Jesus said, "*Neither do I condemn you; go, and from now on sin no more.*"

See the great love of the Lord. He in no way wants the death of the wicked but that the wicked returns and lives. As we read in Ezekiel 33:11:

Ezekiel 33:11
"Say to them, As I live, declares the Lord God, *I have no pleasure in the death of the wicked, but that the wicked turn from his way and live;*

turn back, turn back from your evil ways, for why will you die, O house of Israel?"

This was and is the will of God for the ungodly: He wants him to repent and turn back. He in no way wants his condemnation, his death. This does not mean that He is indifferent to sin. But to the sinner, He says: "I do not condemn you. The past is past. *Go and from now on sin no more*"! Please note here: He does not just say "neither do I condemn you", but also *"go and from now on sin no more"*. Therefore He expects something from the sinner: to go and sin no more. May we be thankful for His forgiveness and instead of taking it for granted, may we take it as it truly is: a new beginning and may we strive to go and from now on sin no more.

## 5.22. THE REAL FAMILY OF JESUS: "THOSE WHO HEAR THE WORD OF GOD AND DO IT"

In Luke 8:20-21 we read how and who Jesus defined to be His brothers and His very own:

Luke 8:20-21
"And it was told to Him by some, who said, Your mother and Your brothers are standing outside desiring to see You. And He answered and said to them, My mother and My brothers are those *who hear the Word of God and do it."*

Those who hear and also do the Word are the brothers of Jesus. As we have repeatedly seen up to now, it is for Jesus *the doing of the Word* that matters. The hearing of the Word should also be followed by acting on what we heard.

## 5.23. 1 CORINTHIANS 5:5: "SO THAT HIS SPIRIT MAY BE SAVED IN THE DAY OF THE LORD"

Moving now to 1 Corinthians 5 and starting from verse 1 we read about some great sexual immorality that was going on in the Corinthian church.

1 Corinthians 5:1-5
"It is actually reported that there is sexual immorality among you, *and of a kind that is not tolerated even among pagans, for a man has his father's wife.* And you are arrogant! Ought you not rather to mourn? Let him who has done this be removed from among you. For though absent in body, I am present in spirit; and as if present, I have already pronounced judgment on the one who did such a thing. When you are assembled in the name of the Lord Jesus and my spirit is present, with the power of our Lord Jesus, you are to deliver this man to Satan for the destruction of the flesh, *so that his spirit may be saved in the day of the Lord.*"

Among whom was there sexual immorality? "Among you", among the believers, Paul says. This immediately tells us that a believer is indeed capable of such things as practicing sexual immorality of the worst kind that even the pagans could not tolerate. Now I would like to ask us the following: would the people who practiced these things and who were obviously "believers", be saved, if they did not repent for what they were practicing? This is a rather rhetorical question as the answer is in the text and the way Paul reacted to the situation. Let's see it again:

1 Corinthians 5:4-5
"When you are assembled in the name of the Lord Jesus and my spirit is present, with the power of our Lord Jesus, you are to deliver this man to Satan for the destruction of the flesh, *so that his spirit may be saved in the day of the Lord.*"

The reason that this man should have been delivered to Satan was to lead him to repentance, through the "destruction of the flesh" that this would bring, "so that his spirit may be saved in the day of the Lord". To say it differently: if the flesh, the old man, of this person was crushed and he repented then his spirit, he himself, would be saved in the day of the Lord. From this it is obvious that if this "destruction of the flesh" would not happen and this person would not repent, then his spirit would not be saved in the day of the Lord. Paul, in order to avoid this and bring repentance, says deliver this man to Satan for the destruction of the flesh. But did those who were practicing such and similar sins finally repent? In 2 Corinthians Paul follows up on the matter of sexual immorality in the Corinthian church. Here is what he says:

2 Corinthians 12:21
"I fear that when I come again my God may humble me before you, and I may have to mourn over *many* of those *who sinned earlier and have not repented of the impurity and fornication and lasciviousness that they have practiced.*"

As we see it was not just one but *many* who were living in impurity, fornication and lasciviousness. As we also see, many of these people had NOT repented and we do not know whether they ever really did.

A couple of things that I would like us to notice concerning these people: what they were doing was not a sin while being on the right way. This was not an episode of sin, but, as the text says, their *practice*, what they did habitually and as a way of life. They were *working* lawlessness to use the words of the Lord (Matthew 7:23). If they would not repent, would they find the door of the Kingdom open and the King waiting for them to welcome them in, just because once upon a time they believed? The answer is no. Because it is clear from Matthew 7:21-23 that the King will not welcome but rather send away those who work lawlessness:

"Not everyone who says to me, 'Lord, Lord,' will enter the kingdom of heaven, but the one who does the will of my Father who is in heaven. On that day many will say to me, 'Lord, Lord, did we not prophesy in your name, and cast out demons in your name, and do many mighty works in your name?' And then will I declare to them, '*I never knew you; depart from me, you workers of lawlessness.*'"

In contrast to many today who have chosen to ignore the above reality, Paul did not ignore it. That is why he was rather upset that the church in Corinth was arrogant and had not taken action to discipline these people so that they might repent and their spirit "may be saved in the day of the Lord".

## 5.24. PETER 2: "IT WOULD HAVE BEEN BETTER FOR THEM NEVER TO HAVE KNOWN THE WAY OF RIGHTEOUSNESS"

I left for last two of the "heaviest" passages in this chapter, which are incidentally similar: 2 Peter 2 and Jude. Let's start from 2 Peter. This epistle has three chapters. The biggest of the three is devoted to the description of some very dangerous people related to the topic we are discussing here. We saw already parts of this chapter in a previous section. But let's read now a big part of it:

2 Peter 2:1-19
"But false prophets also arose among the people, just as there will be false teachers among you, who will secretly bring in destructive heresies, *even denying the Master who bought them, bringing upon themselves swift destruction*. And many will follow their sensuality, and because of them the way of truth will be blasphemed. And in their greed they will exploit you with false words. Their condemnation from long ago is not idle, and their destruction is not asleep. For if God did not spare angels when they sinned, but cast them into hell and committed them to chains of gloomy darkness to be kept until the judgment; if he did not spare the ancient world, but preserved Noah, a herald of righteousness, with seven others, when he brought a flood upon the world of the ungodly; if by turning the cities of Sodom and Gomorrah to ashes he condemned them to extinction, making

them an example of what is going to happen to the ungodly; and if he rescued righteous Lot, greatly distressed by the sensual conduct of the wicked (for as that righteous man lived among them day after day, he was tormenting his righteous soul over their lawless deeds that he saw and heard); then the Lord knows how to rescue the godly from trials, and to keep the unrighteous under punishment until the day of judgment, and especially those who indulge in the lust of defiling passion and despise authority. Bold and willful, they do not tremble as they blaspheme the glorious ones, whereas angels, though greater in might and power, do not pronounce a blasphemous judgment against them before the Lord. But these, like irrational animals, creatures of instinct, born to be caught and destroyed, blaspheming about matters of which they are ignorant, will also be destroyed in their destruction, suffering wrong as the wage for their wrongdoing. They count it pleasure to revel in the daytime. They are blots and blemishes, reveling in their deceptions, while they feast with you. They have eyes full of adultery, insatiable for sin. They entice unsteady souls. They have hearts trained in greed. Accursed children! *Forsaking the right way, they have gone astray.* They have followed the way of Balaam, the son of Beor, who loved gain from wrongdoing, but was rebuked for his own transgression; a speechless donkey spoke with human voice and restrained the prophet's madness. These are waterless springs and mists driven by a storm. For them the gloom of utter darkness has been reserved. For, speaking loud boasts of folly, they entice by sensual passions of the flesh those who are barely escaping from those who live in error. They promise them freedom, but they themselves are slaves of corruption. For whatever overcomes a person, to that he is enslaved."

Many oppose the idea that the people we read about were ever believers. And indeed, up to here somebody may say that it is perhaps not 100% clear whether the people Peter is speaking about were ever Christians, though there are some indications: they denied the Master *who bought them.* Also as we read: *"Forsaking the right way,* they have gone astray". How could somebody forsake the right way if he was never in the right way? Nevertheless, the verses of 2 Peter that follow leave no doubt that these people were once part of the family of the believers but eventually turned back, returning to the defilements of the world:

2 Peter 2:20-22
For if, after *they have escaped the defilements of the world through the knowledge of our Lord and Savior Jesus Christ*, they are again entangled in them and overcome, the last state has become worse for them than the first. For it would have been better for them never *to have known the way of righteousness* than after knowing it to turn back from *the holy commandment delivered to them*. What the true proverb says has happened to them: "The dog returns to its own vomit, and the sow, after washing herself, returns to wallow in the mire."

That these people were once believers is obvious from the following facts:

i) they had escaped the defilements of the world *through the knowledge of our Lord and Savior Jesus Christ.* It speaks about knowing the Lord here and you cannot know Him without faith. Even as believers, knowing the Lord Jesus Christ is an aim and not something that happens automatically.

That these people were once of the family of the believers with personal knowledge of the Lord becomes undeniable by the use of the Greek word "epignosis". This word does not mean just head knowledge or simply knowledge. In contrast it means precise knowledge that is applied in practice. Here is how Vine's dictionary defines this word:

Epignosis: "denotes *"exact or full knowledge,* discernment, recognition," expressing a fuller or a full "knowledge," a greater participation by the "knower" in the object "known," thus more powerfully influencing him" (emphasis added)

Epignosis is the noun form of the verb "epiginosko". About this verb, Vine says:

"it denotes "to observe, *fully perceive, notice attentively*, discern, recognize" and "suggests generally a directive, a more special, recognition of the object "known" than does [ginosko]; it also may suggest *advanced "knowledge"* or special appreciation; thus, in Rom. 1:32, "knowing the ordinance of God" (epiginosko) means *"knowing full well,"* whereas in verse Rom. 1:21 "knowing God" (ginosko) simply suggests that they could not avoid the perception. Sometimes epiginosko implies a special participation in the object "known," and gives greater weight to what is stated; thus in John 8:32, "ye shall know the truth," ginosko is used, whereas in 1 Tim. 4:3, "them that believe and know the truth," *epiginosko lays stress on participation in the truth."* (emphasis added)

An unbeliever may hear about God but if the Word does not enter his heart it will never lead to real knowledge of Jesus Christ, let alone full perception as the word "epignosis" denotes.

Just for the record, here are some examples where the word "epignosis" is used in connection to knowing God and the Lord Jesus Christ:

Ephesians 4:11-14
"And he gave the apostles, the prophets, the evangelists, the shepherds and teachers, to equip the saints for the work of ministry, for building up the body of Christ, until we all attain to the unity of the faith and of the knowledge *[epignosis]* of the Son of God, to mature manhood, to the measure of the stature of the fullness of Christ, so that we may no longer be children, tossed to and fro by the waves and carried about by every wind of doctrine, by human cunning, by craftiness in deceitful schemes."

Ephesians 1:17
"the God of our Lord Jesus Christ, the Father of glory, may give you the Spirit of wisdom and of revelation in the knowledge [epignosis] of him"

Colossians 1:9-10
"And so, from the day we heard, we have not ceased to pray for you, asking that you may be filled with the knowledge [epiginosko] of his will in all spiritual wisdom and understanding,  so as to walk in a manner worthy of the Lord, fully pleasing to him, bearing fruit in every good work and increasing in the knowledge [epignosis] of God."

Colossians 2:1-2
"For I want you to know how great a struggle I have for you and for those at Laodicea and for all who have not seen me face to face, that their hearts may be encouraged, being knit together in love, to reach all the riches of full assurance of understanding and the knowledge [epignosis] of God's mystery, which is Christ."

Colossians 3:9-10
"Do not lie to one another, seeing that you have put off the old self with its practices and have put on the new self, which is being renewed in knowledge [epignosis] after the image of its creator."

2 Timothy 2:24-25
"And the Lord's servant must not be quarrelsome but kind to everyone, able to teach, patiently enduring evil, correcting his opponents with gentleness. God may perhaps grant them repentance leading to a knowledge [epignosis] of the truth"

I think that we could not seriously support that any of these passages referring to knowing (epignosis) God and His Son could also apply to unbelievers. I wonder though why then some so fiercely oppose the idea that these people of 2 Peter were once believers, when it is so clearly written in the Word that they go back to the defilements of the world, *after* they had initially escaped them "through the *knowledge [epignosis]* of our Lord and Savior Jesus Christ", the same knowledge that is the aim and the prayer for all of us, the believers? I would instruct us instead of fighting what is clearly written in the Word of God in order to support whatever cherished doctrines we may have, to submit to the Word accepting it like little children, especially since to Him, to the living Word of God, we will one day give account.

ii) That these people in 2 Peter were once believers is also obvious by the fact that, "the holy commandment was delivered unto them". Could a holy commandment ever be delivered to unbelievers? I do not think so. Speaking about commandment brings to my mind what Paul said to Timothy:

1 Timothy 6:12-14:
"Fight the good fight of the faith. Take hold of the eternal life to which you were called and about which you made the good confession in the presence of many witnesses. I charge you in the presence of God, who gives life to all things, and of Christ Jesus, who in his testimony before Pontius Pilate made the good confession, to *keep the commandment unstained* and free from reproach until the appearing of our Lord Jesus Christ"

Really, why would Paul charge Timothy to keep the commandment unstained if it was impossible that he would ever stain it?

Back to those of 2 Peter: they were recipients of the "holy commandment", which in a broad sense I take to mean the Word of God and what it commands us. As for example 1 John 3:23 tells us:

"And this is his *commandment*, that we believe in the name of his Son Jesus Christ and love one another, just as he has *commanded* us."

Furthermore, these people also got to know the way of righteousness. Again the word "know" is a translation of the Greek word "epiginosko" i.e. it is not a simple knowledge that is meant but a rather deep and good knowledge of the way of righteousness. Could this really happen to people that are not believers? No it could not. What I believe the above facts very clearly say is that these people belonged originally to the family of the believers, but then they apostatized from the faith. To apostatize means to belong somewhere and then betray it, turning back, moving away from it. Such apostates were also those of 2 Peter 2.

What will the end of these people be? The answer is in the following parts of 2 Peter 2:

"For it would have been *better for them never to have known the way of righteousness* than after knowing it to turn back from the holy commandment delivered to them."

and:

"bringing upon themselves *swift destruction*"

## 5.25. JUDE: "TURNING THE GRACE OF OUR GOD INTO LASCIVIOUSNESS" - A MUCH RELEVANT WARNING

Jude is a very short epistle, just 25 verses all in all. But it is both powerful and with an evident urgency. Verse 3 starts right away on the subject:

Jude 3
"Beloved, although I was very eager to write to you about our common salvation, I found it necessary to write appealing to you to contend for the faith that was once for all delivered to the saints."

The "faith that was once for all delivered to the saints" was in danger and the believers had to fight, to contend, for it. What was wrong, what was happening? The next verse says it:

Jude 4
"For certain people have crept in unnoticed who long ago were designated for this condemnation, ungodly people, *who pervert the grace of our God into lasciviousness and deny our only Master and Lord, Jesus Christ.*"

These people were doing two things:

1. They were perverting the grace of our God into lasciviousness.
2. They were denying our only Master and Lord Jesus Christ.

But how did they do that? As Jude says: they had *crept in unnoticed*. This then indicates that they were not explicitly and loudly saying that "Jesus Christ is neither our Lord nor our Master". Else they would immediately be noticed. Instead they "crept in unnoticed", perhaps by transforming themselves the same way Paul says that the servants of Satan transform themselves into ministers of righteousness:

2 Corinthians 11:13-15
"For such are false apostles, deceitful workers, *transforming themselves into the apostles of Christ.* And no marvel; for Satan himself is transformed into an angel of light. Therefore *it is no great thing if his ministers also be transformed as the ministers of righteousness; whose end shall be according to their works.*"

Satan's workers are not coming, presenting themselves as wolves, because then they would be noticed. Instead they come camouflaged as sheep. They appear as "ministers of righteousness", but their very works show that they are *not*.

The fruit, the life that somebody lives, what he is practicing is the clearest and I would say the only true indicator of whether he is a real sheep or a real wolf in sheep's clothing. The Lord said this very clearly in Matthew 7:15-20:

"Beware of false prophets, who come to you in sheep's clothing but inwardly are ravenous wolves. *You will recognize them by their fruits.* Are grapes gathered from thornbushes, or figs from thistles? So, every healthy tree bears good fruit, but the diseased tree bears bad fruit. A healthy tree cannot bear bad fruit, nor can a diseased tree bear good fruit. Every tree that does not bear good fruit is cut down and thrown into the fire. *Therefore by their fruits you will know them.* "

Despite the camouflage, the fruit, the works of these people – and not the sheep's clothing they are wearing - is the unmistakable indicator of whose servants they truly are.

In addition , as Jude 12 says: "these are hidden reefs at your love feasts, as they feast with you without fear". In other words these people were taking part in the common meals – the love feasts - the believers were having as a church.

Now let's summarize:

i) These people had crept in unnoticed. This indicates that they had camouflaged themselves to look like sheep while in fact they were ravenous wolves.

ii) They were participating together with the true believers in the common meals they were having as a church.

iii) the believers had no idea that these were really wolves and the danger they posed. If they knew the danger, they would already be contending for the true faith once delivered to the saints and there would be no need for Jude to urgently ask them to do so.

I believe these facts tell us that these false teachers were presenting themselves as Christians. In fact Jude is very similar to 2 Peter 2, which also speaks about false teachers who, before they turned away becoming false teachers, were indeed of the family of the believers. I do not know whether they both speak about exactly the same situation but the only way I see that these people got unnoticed, despite the corruption they were spreading, is by posing themselves as Christians.

Turning into what they were doing, they were: perverting the grace of God into lasciviousness and denying our only Lord and Master Jesus Christ. Let's now get into each of these.

## "Perverting the grace of God into lasciviousness"

Concerning the word lasciviousness, this is a translation of the Greek word "aselgeia". This word is used 10 times in the New Testament and shows up in the related lists of the works of the flesh (see Mark 7:21-22, Romans 13:13, Galatians 5:19-21). According to Vine's dictionary it denotes:

"excess, licentiousness, absence of restraint, indecency, wantonness;"

Perhaps the NIV has the best translation of Jude 1:4 when it says:

"They are ungodly people, *who pervert the grace of our God into a license for immorality*".

These people had perverted the grace of God into a license for immorality. But how did they do this? I believe through perverted teaching, in word and in deed. In the "grace" they were teaching there was also a place for living in lasciviousness and sin. Was somebody living in sin? Well, not such of a problem. Their "grace" covered also this. It is difficult to understand what was happening exactly and I do not want to read more into the text than what it really says, but it is a fact and written in the text that they were indeed perverting the grace into a license for immorality, sin.

110

## "Denying our only Lord and Master Jesus Christ"

Furthermore, it is written in the text that these people were denying our only Lord and Master Jesus Christ. The word translated as "Master" is the Greek word "Despotes", from which the English word "Despot" derives. It means absolute Lord. In other words, Jude is using two very similar words, one of them very strong, to point out the absolute Lordship of Jesus Christ, which these people were denying.

But can it really be? Can such people creep into the church, fellowship with the believers, practically deny the Lordship of Jesus Christ, pervert the grace of God into a license for immorality and yet get unnoticed? Unfortunately it can happen. In fact I believe it happens today. Many are those today who teach a message of cheap grace. A grace according to which Jesus is more our servant than Lord. A grace in which somebody is saved once and for all the minute he believed and what he will do after that minute, whether he will stay in the faith, whether he will stay in the vine, in Christ, is not that relevant. What is relevant is that moment of faith. The beginning rather than the end. Do you want to live according to the world? It would be good not to do it, they may tell you, but if you do it, it is not that of a problem! The grace is grace! To summarize it in one phrase: you can, according to them, to be the following oxymoron: a Christian but not a disciple of Christ. But as Acts 11:26 tells us:

"and in Antioch *the disciples* were first called Christians"

It is the disciples that were called Christians. To tell it differently: there is no such thing as Christians who are not disciples of Christians. Whoever is not a disciple, a follower of Christ, is not a Christian.

As the German theologian Dietrich Bonhoeffer summarized it:

"cheap grace is the preaching of forgiveness without requiring repentance ... Cheap grace is grace without discipleship, grace without the cross, grace without Jesus Christ."

Unfortunately such is the grace that many teach and their teaching has been very popular. It is however a fake grace, a distortion of the true grace of God and we should be alerted so that we do not fall victims of it. And as Peter closes his second epistle:

2 Peter 3:17-18
"You therefore, beloved, knowing this beforehand, take care that you are not carried away with the error of lawless people and lose your own stability. But grow in the grace and knowledge of our Lord and Savior Jesus Christ. To him be the glory both now and to the day of eternity. Amen."

# 6

## DO WE LOSE OUR SALVATION EVERY TIME WE SIN?

Some people claim that once a person sins then he loses his salvation and he needs to repent, till he sins again and then loses his salvation again and so on. I do not think that this is so. We can be in the faith and unfortunately sin, stumble (but still be on the way) and then get up and move on. As 1 John says:

1 John 1:5-10
"This is the message we have heard from him and proclaim to you, that God is light, and in him is no darkness at all. If we say we have fellowship with him while we walk in darkness, we lie and do not practice the truth. *But if we walk in the light, as he is in the light, we have fellowship with one another, and the blood of Jesus his Son cleanses us from all sin.* If we say we have no sin, we deceive ourselves, and the truth is not in us. If we confess our sins, he is faithful and just to forgive us our sins and to cleanse us from all unrighteousness. If we say we have not sinned, we make him a liar, and his word is not in us. My little children, I am writing these things to you so that you may not sin. But if anyone does sin, we have an advocate with the Father, Jesus Christ the righteous. He is the propitiation for our sins, and not for ours only but also for the sins of the whole world."

I want to point out verse 7: *"But if we walk in the light,* as he is in the light, we have fellowship with one another, and the blood of Jesus his Son cleanses us from all sin." Why would there be any need for the blood of Christ to cleanse us from any sin since we are walking in the light? It seems to me that walking in the light does not necessarily mean that we are not going to sin. What I mean is that sin is a possibility also in this case, but it is an "episode", something that we put behind us and move on. We are not practicing sin; we are not living in sin. It comes on our way and rather easily[8] but we do not practice it i.e. do it willingly, habitually and as a way of life. And as we confess our sins the blood of Christ cleanses us from all of them.

Now walking in the light is one scenario but not the only one for a believer. There is another one also and this is walking in the darkness. As the apostle said:

"If we say we have fellowship with him while *we walk in darkness,* we lie and do not *practice the truth."*

"Practice the truth" is something that stands out for me here. When we walk in the darkness we do not *practice* the truth, which turned the other way around also reads: when we do not practice the truth then we walk in the darkness. 1 John 2:9-11 gives a direct application of the above:

1 John 2:9-11
"Whoever says he is in the light and hates his brother is still in *darkness.* Whoever loves his brother abides in the light, and in him there is no cause for stumbling. But whoever hates his brother is

---

[8] As Hebrews 12:1 says: "let us lay aside every weight, and the sin which **so easily ensnares us**". The phrase "so easily ensnares us" is one word in the Greek text, the word "euperispaston". According to Barnes: "it properly means, "standing well around;" and hence, denotes what is near, or at hand, or readily occurring. So Chrysostom explains it. .. Tyndale renders it "the sin that hangeth on us."

in the darkness and walks in the darkness, and does not know where he is going, because the darkness has blinded his eyes."

and 1 John 4:20
"If anyone says, "I love God," and hates his brother, *he is a liar*; for he who does not love his brother whom he has seen cannot love God whom he has not seen."

Furthermore, 1 John 3:14-15
"We know that we have passed out of death into life, because we love the brothers. Whoever does not love *abides in death*. Everyone who hates his brother is a murderer, and you know that *no murderer has eternal life abiding in him.*"

We see here what we have seen in all previous cases: as far as the Bible is concerned, it is not that important what we say that we are but what our fruit shows that we really are i.e. what we are practicing. As Apostle John says: somebody who hates his brother is a murderer and has no eternal life abiding in him. If he says he loves God, John says, do not believe him, for if he does not love his brother whom he saw, how can he love God whom he has not seen? Now let me ask something: do we, based on the above, really think that a brother hater who has not repented, i.e. an unrepentant murderer, will end up in the Kingdom of God, just because he says he loves God, and because he is a "brother" (that is how he is called)? I believe the answer of John is a clear no. "No murderer has eternal life abiding in him" he tells us, and the context does not speak about heathen murderers but Christians that hate their brothers. I believe in the Kingdom there will be many repented murderers, but there will not be even a single unrepentant one.

As Paul warns in Galatians 5:19-21:

Galatians 5:19-21
"Now the works of the flesh are evident: sexual immorality, impurity, sensuality,  idolatry, sorcery, enmity, strife, jealousy, fits of anger, rivalries, dissensions, divisions,  envy, drunkenness,

orgies, and things like these. *I warn you, as I warned you before, that those who do such things will not inherit the kingdom of God."*

The Greek word translated as "do" (in the "do such things" phrase) is the word "prasso", from which we get in English the verb "to practice". According to Strong's dictionary it means, among others:

*"to "practice", that is, perform repeatedly or habitually"*.

Now why would Paul need to warn the Galatian believers that those who practice these things will not enter into the Kingdom (that is what "inherit the Kingdom" means – just do a search on the word "inherit" in the New Testament and it will become evident), if they were already in the Kingdom from the moment they believed, regardless of what happened after that? Obviously, if this was really so, he would have no reason to give them this warning. But he did, which means there was a reason for this. And the reason is very simple: whether we live out our faith, whether we practice it or not practice it, proves really whether we are really in the faith or not. To say it differently: those who say they are believers (and perhaps once they were true believers), yet habitually and repeatedly practice sin by hating their brother (which is equal to murder) or by practicing any of the other things described in Galatians 5:19-21 and do not repent of this behavior, will find the door of the Kingdom shut. They will not inherit the Kingdom of God Paul said. Also Hebrews 10:26-27 is very clear:

"For if we *sin willfully* after that we have received the knowledge of the truth, *there no longer remains a sacrifice for sins, but a fearful expectation of judgment, and a fury of fire that will consume the adversaries."*

Going back now to 1 John 1:5-7 and reading it again:

1 John 1:5-7
"This is the message we have heard from him and proclaim to you, that God is light, and in him is no darkness at all. If we say we have fellowship with him while *we walk in darkness*, we lie and do not practice the truth. But if *we walk in the light*, as he is in the light, we have fellowship with one another, and the blood of Jesus his Son cleanses us from all sin."

There is walking in the light and walking in the darkness. Those who walk in the light may fall here and there but they do *not* practice – habitually, repeatedly and as a way of life - sin. Instead they habitually and repeatedly (as a way of life) practice the truth i.e. they strive to live what the Word of God says in practice. They may sin here and there but they are on the way. They will find the door of the Kingdom open.

In contrast to these, there are those who walk in the darkness, and this means they practice sin, repeatedly and habitually. Sin is their way of life. These are walking in darkness and their fruit is the proof of this. If they do not repent they will find the door of the Kingdom shut.

So, it is not sinning while walking in the light that marks that somebody is out of the faith  but sinning as a way of life; practicing sin willfully and habitually. However, we should be careful here as all habits have a start. Therefore, if we fell and sinned let us not take it with a light heart but after we confess it to the Lord let us be alerted, lest we give place to sin and then what was just an episode becomes a habit.

# 7

## COMMON OBJECTIONS

Since I was one of those who was taught the view that salvation is something received once and for all the moment somebody believes and regardless of what happens after that, I know very well some of the arguments people use to support it. Here are some that I have heard:

### 7.1. I AM A CHILD OF GOD AND THIS CANNOT BE CHANGED.

This argument goes as follows: "I am a son of God, a child of God and this cannot be taken away. That second I believed, I was born again and the deal was sealed. I am saved regardless of what I do in my life. Can a son ever stop to be a son?"

My comment
This argument uses the analogy of the physical sonship according to which "once a son always a son". But really what is the validity of this argument in the spiritual ground? For example angels are also called sons of God in the Bible. All of them, including also the fallen ones (Genesis 6:2) and even Satan himself (Job 2:1)! Does that mean that all of them are still, *effectively*, *really*, *now* sons of God in the meaning of having fellowship and enjoying what God has for those who are truly of His household?

No! In Genesis 6 we read about angels that apostatized. They are in the abyss now, in a prison of darkness waiting for the day of judgment (2 Peter 2:4). Can Satan expect anything other than his utter destruction, just because he was once an angel of light? No, he cannot. In addition: did the fact that those were children of God - as Adam also was - prohibit them from falling and ending up - as they will do - in the lake of fire? No it did not. So why is it that some of us consider that being a child of God, because we once believed, actually means that we have no obligations and we can also be a prodigal son and still have the father taking us back, *without us repenting and returning to Him*? Remember the father in the parable of the prodigal son: he received his son back with joy! But when? *When he repented and came back home.* He could have chosen to continue living without repenting and finally die alone somewhere. But he did not do this. Instead he repented, he returned home and this made the whole difference. Concerning us, Paul clarifies:

Romans 8:12-14
"So then, brothers, we are debtors, not to the flesh, to live according to the flesh. For if you live according to the flesh you will die, but if by the Spirit you put to death the deeds of the body, you will live. *For as many as are led by the Spirit of God, they are the sons of God.*"

We became children of God by faith in Jesus Christ (Galatians 3:26). But then why does the same apostle say here: "for as many as are led by the spirit of God, they are the sons of God"? What does it mean to be led by the spirit of God? It means to be driven by the Spirit, by the new nature, to walk by the Spirit, to walk by the new nature, to strive to do the will of God, to abide in the vine and to have His Word abiding in us. Can somebody be led by the Spirit of God, when God's Word does not abide in him? Can somebody walk by the Spirit, if he does not abide in the vine, in Christ? No, he cannot. So what Paul essentially tells us here, is that *real* children of God are those who are led not by the flesh, the old nature, but by the new nature, the Spirit, Christ in us. We also saw previously, in Luke 8:20-21, Jesus making this clear when He said:

"And he was told, "Your mother and your brothers are standing outside, desiring to see you." But he answered them, "My mother and *my brothers are those who hear the word of God and do it.*"

Real children of God, real brothers and sisters of Jesus Christ are those who hear the Word of God *and do it*. People who have discontinued in the faith, people who run after the world, its riches, pleasures and cares or turned back because of tribulation and temptation, in short, people who no longer abide in the vine, in Christ, are clearly excluded from those that Jesus, and also Paul in Romans, consider as real children of God. What should then somebody do if he is in that category? The answer is repentance and return to our loving Father. The parable of the prodigal son is here a good example:

Luke 15:20-24
"And he arose and came to his father. But while he was still a long way off, his father saw him and felt compassion, and ran and embraced him and kissed him. And the son said to him, 'Father, I have sinned against heaven and before you. I am no longer worthy to be called your son.' But the father said to his servants, 'Bring quickly the best robe, and put it on him, and put a ring on his hand, and shoes on his feet. And bring the fattened calf and kill it, and let us eat and celebrate. For this my son was dead, and is alive again; he was lost, and is found.' And they began to celebrate."

## 7.2. "NO ONE CAN SNATCH ME OUT OF JESUS' HAND" (JOHN 10:27-28)

I have heard people using this passage from John to support that they will never be snatched out of Jesus' hand, *regardless* of whether they really follow Jesus or not, as long as they once upon a time believed in Jesus. But is this what the Word of God says? Let's please read this passage in its context:

John 10:27-29
*"My sheep hear my voice, and I know them, and they follow me.* I give them eternal life, and they will never perish, and no one will snatch them out of my hand. My Father, who has given them to me, is greater than all, and no one is able to snatch them out of the Father's hand."

The promise of "I give them eternal life and they will never perish and no one will snatch them out of my hand" is made for those of verse 27:

*"My sheep hear my voice, and I know them, and they follow me"*

To be a sheep of Christ and to be included in the promise of verse 28 we have to hear His voice, to be known by Him and to follow Him. Now let's unpack this a bit more. What does it mean to follow Christ? Does it mean to just, in time past, make a confession of faith and from there on one is included automatically and forever to those who follow Him? Is really somebody who though he believed that Jesus is the Son of God, then turned back to the world living after the flesh, covered by the promise of John 10:27-29? Does such a person really follow Christ? Well let's allow the Master to explain what it takes to follow Him:

Luke 9:23-24
"And he said to all, "If anyone would come after me, *let him deny himself and take up his cross daily and follow me.* For whoever would save his life will lose it, but whoever loses his life for my sake will save it."

And also: Matthew 10:38
"And *whoever does not take his cross and follow me is not worthy of me."*

To follow Christ we need to take up our cross and go behind Him. Following implies moving. Following Christ is something dynamic, something that implies moving, and in fact moving behind somebody else, the Lord. It is a daily business ( "take up his cross *daily* and follow me" ) The first moment of faith is on the other hand something static, something which happened at a certain point in time. This moment put us behind Christ. Now we have to follow Him. This moment brought us into the faith. Now we have to run with patience the race of faith to the end, looking unto Jesus the leader of our faith.  As we read in 1 John:

1 John 2:10-11
"*Whoever loves his brother abides in the light*, and in him there is no cause for stumbling. But *whoever hates his brother is in the darkness and walks in the darkness*, and does not know where he is going, because the darkness has blinded his eyes."

John does not say that because we once believed we walk automatically in the light and follow Jesus forever and ever. Instead, following Jesus is something to be done daily. People who, for example, hate their brothers are walking in the darkness and they are *not* followers of Jesus, regardless of their once upon a time faith. Since they are not followers of Jesus they are not of His sheep, for His sheep hear His voice and *follow Him*. Can we then say that the promise of John 10:28: "I give them eternal life, and they will never perish, and no one will snatch them out of my hand" applies to them and whoever else walks in the darkness, without repenting? No, we cannot, for this promise is to those who follow Him. For people who are willing to lose their life in order to find it. Yes, such people nobody can snatch out of Jesus' hand.

## 7.3. "GOD WILL PRESENT ME BLAMELESS ANYWAY, REGARDLESS OF WHAT I DO."

Another one of the passages used to support the same view is also Jude 1:24. There we read:

Jude 1:24-25

"Now to him who is able to keep you from stumbling and to present you blameless before the presence of his glory with great joy, to the only God, our Savior, through Jesus Christ our Lord, be glory, majesty, dominion, and authority, before all time and now and forever. Amen."

So people basically say: "you see, God is able to keep me from stumbling and to present me blameless". Thus, they conclude, "it does not really matter what I do. God will present me blameless anyway". But this is clearly a misinterpretation of the passage. And to understand this better, again we have to take the context into account. So let's read it:

Jude 1:20-25

"But you, beloved, building yourselves up in your most holy faith and praying in the Holy Spirit, *keep yourselves in the love of God*, waiting for the mercy of our Lord Jesus Christ that leads to eternal life. And have mercy on those who doubt; save others by snatching them out of the fire; to others show mercy with fear, hating even the garment stained by the flesh. Now *to him who is able to keep you* from stumbling and to present you blameless before the presence of his glory with great joy, to the only God, our Savior, through Jesus Christ our Lord, be glory, majesty, dominion, and authority, before all time and now and forever. Amen."

"Keep yourselves in the love of God" Jude says. If his understanding was that we will be kept anyway by God, regardless of what we practice, why does he tell us to keep ourselves in the love of God? If there is no possibility to NOT keep ourselves in His love, to not continue in His kindness, then there would be no point for the instruction. In a similar tone Peter said:

2 Peter 3:17
"Therefore, beloved, knowing beforehand, *beware lest being led away with the error of the lawless, you fall from your own steadfastness."*

Is there a possibility that a "beloved", a true believer, be led away and fall from being steadfast for the Lord? Yes there is. That is why we should beware. Who is to beware, be alerted? Who is to keep himself in the love of God? Will God do this for us or we do this? It is clear that we do this. Will God help us in this? Of course! He will help us to be kept, if we really want to be kept. How are we then to understand Jude 1:24? We are not to understand it as God coercing people not to fall away but as God helping people who want to keep themselves in the love of God to actually do it. If we want to be kept in the love of God, He will help us to do so and we will for sure succeed. But if somebody does not want to continue with Him any longer, God will not force him to continue.

## 7.4. "HE WHO STARTED THE GOOD WORK IN ME WILL FINISH IT ANYWAY"

Philippians 1:6 is another passage used to support that once somebody believes, there is no way he will ever fall away. Here is what the passage says:

"Being confident of this very thing, that He who has begun a good work in you will perform it until the day of Jesus Christ,"

So some people take this passage and say: "God started the work and he will perform it till the end" and implicitly add to this: "regardless of what I do". It is similar argument to the one we saw used in Jude 1:24. And as in Jude 1:24 and earlier in John 10:28, so also here the context is ignored. However before we see the context, I would like to point out that Paul speaks about confidence. Being confident for something means that I believe something and I believe it strongly, but it does not mean that I am 100% sure about it. I am confident about it. Now moving on, why was Paul confident? Was he as confident regarding everybody, every Christian, as he was of the Philippians? If it was just the fact that they believed once upon a time, that made him so confident, then he would have been just as confident about everybody who believed. But he was not. Compare the above confidence regarding the Philippians with the below feedback to the Galatians:

Galatians 4:11
*"I am afraid* I have labored over you *in vain"*

Instead of being confident, he was afraid. Instead of a finished work, he speaks about a labor in vain, wasted. Both the Galatians and the Philippians were believers. But the confidence is not the same concerning both, which in turn shows that Paul's confidence was not simply because once upon a time these people believed and therefore it was sure that God would finish the work in them, regardless of what they did. Why then was Paul so confident about the Philippians? We only need to read the next verse to find out. So verse 7 tells us:

Philippians 1:7
"It is right for me to feel this way about you all, *because* I hold you in my heart, *for* you are all partakers with me of grace, both in my imprisonment and in the defense and confirmation of the gospel."

Barnes expands the above passage as follows:
"There is a reason why I should cherish this hope of you, and this confident expectation that you will be saved. That reason is found in the evidence which you have given that you are sincere

126

Christians. Having evidence of that, it is proper that I should believe that you will finally reach heaven."

Paul saw the fruit of these believers and because of this he was confident that they would continue like this. His confidence is like the confidence you have when you know somebody and you are satisfied with what he does. This is the confidence that Paul had about these believers: he knew them, he had seen their fruit and he was confident that they would be there at the end. He was confident that they would keep themselves in the love of God and God, who is able to keep them from stumbling, would finish the work that He had started in them. I believe this is a more accurate way to understand this passage. If we use it to say "God will finish the work in me, regardless of whether or not I hold fast to his Word or keep myself in His love", then we abuse it.

In fact Paul, with all the confidence he had about the Philippians, kept instructing them:

Philippians 2:12-16
"Therefore, my beloved, as you have always obeyed, so now, not only as in my presence but much more in my absence, *work out your own salvation with fear and trembling*, for it is God who works in you, both to will and to work for his good pleasure. Do all things without grumbling or disputing, that you may be blameless and innocent, children of God without blemish in the midst of a crooked and twisted generation, among whom you shine as lights in the world, *holding fast to the word of life, so that in the day of Christ I may be proud that I did not run in vain or labor in vain*."

In short: Paul's confidence was because of the fruit the Philippians demonstrated. It was not an abstract confidence for everybody. And he exhorts even these fruitful Philippians to hold fast to the Word, which in turn means that there was a possibility – despite all Paul's confidence – that they would not. In that case his labor would be in vain.

## 7.5. "I CAN DO WHATEVER I WANT AND STILL BE SAVED! ON THE DAY OF JUDGMENT MY (SINFUL) WORKS MAY BE BURNED BUT I WILL STILL MAKE IT!"

People get this idea by misinterpreting and taking 1 Corinthians 3:15 again out of context. Let's read this passage in its context:

1 Corinthians 3:10-15
"According to the grace of God given to me, like a skilled master builder I laid a foundation, and someone else is building upon it. Let each one take care how he builds upon it. *For no one can lay a foundation other than that which is laid, which is Jesus Christ.* Now if anyone *builds on the foundation* with gold, silver, precious stones, wood, hay, straw — each one's work will become manifest, for the Day will disclose it, because it will be revealed by fire, and the fire will test what sort of work each one has done. If *the work that anyone has built on the foundation* survives, he will receive a reward. *If anyone's work is burned up, he will suffer loss, though he himself will be saved, but only as through fire.*"

People take verse 15 and think in the back of their mind: "it does not basically matter what I do. Whatever I do, even if I walk according to the flesh, I may lose the rewards but I will still make it into the Kingdom. My works will be burned but I am not in danger." Yet, this is not at all what the passage says. The passage is not speaking about works in general, including sinful works. What it speaks about is building *on the foundation, which is no other than Jesus Christ* i.e. it speaks about works that were done on the foundation of Christ. Therefore, this is not a passage addressed to people who left this foundation to follow the world, living after the flesh, the old nature, and sinning willingly and as a way of life. For this case there are other passages which we have seen in this study. In contrast this passage refers to people who stay in Jesus and have Jesus as their foundation. Not every work that a believer does, will stand the test of fire. Some of them will be burned. Whoever has served God for some time, can probably

128

list some things he has done on the foundation of Christ that will not stand the test of fire. For example, to those who teach the Word, James says:

James 3:1-2
"Not many of you should become teachers, my brothers, for you know that we who teach *will be judged with greater strictness*. [KJV: "we shall receive the greater condemnation"].  For *we all stumble in many ways*. And if anyone does not stumble in what he says, he is a perfect man, able also to bridle his whole body."

Many want to teach the Word of God and if this is what God has called somebody to do, he should do it with fear of God. But this does not mean that it is risk free. There will be a judgment for what one teaches and for any other work built on the foundation: "for the Day will disclose it, because it will be revealed by fire, and the fire will test what sort of work each one has done. If *the work that anyone has built on the foundation* survives, he will receive a reward. *If anyone's work is burned up, he will suffer loss, though he himself will be saved, but only as through fire*." This is the context of the passage. We can apply it for works built on the foundation of Jesus Christ. Some of them are of gold, silver and precious stones, but others of wood, hay and straw. These latter ones will be burned.

## 7.6. SPEAKING IN TONGUES (FOR THOSE OF YOU THAT DO)

This argument goes like this: "I have spoken in tongues. This proves that I have holy spirit and proves that I am saved. If I live in sin and yet speak in tongues, then this proves that despite the life that I live and what I practice I will make it into the Kingdom!"

My comment

The Bible does not say anywhere that whoever spoke in tongues or even did miracles will automatically enter into the Kingdom. In contrast, it says that those who do the will of God, those who keep the faith to the end, will enter. As the Lord said:

"On that day many will say to me, 'Lord, Lord, did we not prophesy in your name, and cast out demons in your name, and do many mighty works in your name?' And then will I declare to them, 'I never knew you; depart from me, you workers of lawlessness."

The Lord does not mention speaking in tongues in his list. It was not available when He was speaking. It became available after Pentecost. He mentions however prophesying, casting out demons and doing mighty works in His name. All these are manifestations of the Spirit, exactly as speaking in tongues is (1 Corinthians 12:1-12). As He said: those who gloried in their prophesying in His name, or in the mighty works they did or in the casting out of demons they performed, yet were practicing, working, lawlessness would not enter into the Kingdom. Therefore if somebody lives in sin he should not glory in speaking in tongues. The Lord warned us that arguments of this type will *not* stand before Him that day. In contrast, he should repent and instead of lawlessness strive with patience to practice the will of God.

There are perhaps other passages used for support by those who believe the view that one is once and for all saved the moment he believes and regardless of what happens to his faith after that. But the explanation is more or less the same as the ones given above: either it is a promise that is made to people who, now in the present, are believers, or the context of the passage is ignored.

# 8

## WHAT SHALL WE DO THEN NOW? SERVE THE LORD!

Closing this study, the question may be: and now what do I do? I believe that the first thing one should do is to take his New Testament and start a careful reading of the gospels and then of the epistles and Revelation, without the glasses of familiar and cherished doctrines, confirming for himself what we saw in this study. As the Bereans were checking Paul from the Scriptures, so you should do also concerning the material in this study.

In addition I would like to present, as a conclusion, the following to you: The Lord is called Lord because He is the Master, the Boss, the one who commands. We, on the other hand, having made Him our Lord are by definition His servants. In fact the word servant in the New Testament has more the meaning of a slave i.e. the meaning of somebody who is completely devoted to doing the will of His Master. As Romans 6:20-23 tells us:

Romans 6:20-23
"For when you were *slaves of sin*, you were free in regard to righteousness. But what fruit were you getting at that time from the things of which you are now ashamed? For the end of those

things is death. But now that you have been set free from sin and have become *slaves of God*, the fruit you get leads to sanctification and its end, eternal life. For the wages of sin is death, but the free gift of God is eternal life in Christ Jesus our Lord."

Before we believed we were slaves of sin. But after believing and being set free from sin we have become *slaves of God*. This is not reserved for some special ones who make a special commitment to the Lord, but for everyone who has made Jesus His Lord. For by making Him his Lord he has simultaneously made himself the servant of this Lord. And here is what the Lord said about those who serve Him, keeping the Master's word and commandments:

John 12:26
"If anyone serves me, he must follow me; and where I am, there will my servant be also. *If anyone serves me, the Father will honor him.*"

John 14:21
"Whoever has my commandments and keeps them, he it is who loves me. And he who loves me will be loved by my Father, *and I will love him and manifest myself to him.*"

John 14:23
"Jesus answered him, "If anyone loves me, he will keep my word, and *my Father will love him, and we will come to him and make our home with him.*"

Speaking about the one that serves Him and keeps what He, the Master, says (i.e. His Word, His commandments, what the Master commands) the Lord said that: "The Father will love him", "the Father will honor him", "I will love him and manifest myself to him", "Me and my Father will come and make our home in him". Wow!!! The phrase "to have fellowship with God" has ended up to be used as a cliché, a phrase that we hear countless times but whose meaning is left vague. But what we read above is not at all vague. Christian life is indeed fellowship with God and having the Father and the Son making their home in us. Having the Son manifesting Himself to us, is the very definition of this fellowship. This is nothing abstract but something that will indeed happen. But to whom? To those who serve God and carry out His Word and will. If we do not care about this will, if we do not consider ourselves slaves of God but rather "believers" who can carry on as being slaves to sin, no such fellowship will be realized. The Lord is very clear: those who love him are those who keep His commandments, His Word. Those who do not do this, they do not love him and the Lord will not manifest Himself to them.

What should we do then? We should make a commitment to follow Jesus, to be His faithful servants, whatever it takes, whatever the cost, living then our lives no more as slaves of sin but as slaves of God.

To avoid misunderstanding: this does not mean running around like panicking chickens, doing whatever comes to our head as the will of God. It rather means checking His Word and finding out what He wants us to do and at the same time be in tune with Him to hear further instructions and commands from the indwelling Master, through the holy spirit in us. Such commands and instructions, if they come from the Master, will *never* violate the written Word of God but will give us direction and wisdom about specific things that God may want us to do and which are not described in detail in the Bible.

See for example the instruction that Paul received to go and preach the Word in Macedonia. He and his team were seeking God on the matter of where to go next and the Master gave them His command, through His indwelling Spirit (Acts 16:6-10). They then as slaves of the Master carried out His will. It is the Master's job to call His servant and the servant's job to be tuned in with the Master so that when He calls, he immediately reacts, carrying out His will.

Do we know the will of God as this is written in the Bible? Are we tuned in with the Master to receive further instructions from Him concerning what He may want us to do? Have we made a commitment to follow the Master no matter what, no matter the cost? If not may be now it is the time to do it.

# APPENDIX 1

## THE PRESENT TENSE IN ANCIENT GREEK. A DEMONSTRATION USING JOHN 3:16

John 3:16 is perhaps one of the most frequently quoted passages, especially when it comes to salvation. Here is the passage together with some of its context:

John 3:14-18
"And as Moses lifted up the serpent in the wilderness, so must the Son of Man be lifted up, that *whoever believes in him may have eternal life*. "For God so loved the world, that he gave his only Son, that *whoever believes in him should not perish but have eternal life*. For God did not send his Son into the world to condemn the world, but in order that the world might be saved through him. *Whoever believes in him is not condemned*, but whoever does not believe is condemned already, because he has not believed in the name of the only Son of God."

Three times in the above five verses we meet the phrase "whoever believes in him", followed by a wonderful promise. Just taking the most popular of these verses, John 3:16, we learn that "whoever *believes* in him should not perish but have eternal life". See that the word "believes" here is in the present tense, denoting something that is a reality now. Many however, read the passage as if it says: "whoever believed" i.e. once in the past. This is obviously not what the passage says. This passage, as well as those seen in the first chapter of this study, is in the *present* tense. Therefore, such passages speak about something that is happening *now*, about a *present*, an *active*, state and not about something that happened once in the past. They speak about a present reality instead of a past history.

In fact it is worth mentioning some facts concerning the present tense in Greek. The website http://www.ntgreek.net/present.htm has an abundance of information on the matter, with lots of references and examples. The basic conclusion (you can check it out in the above or in other similar scholarly websites) is the following: as a rule, the present tense in ancient Greek denotes *duration*. It can also denote something that is happening currently in the present and will not happen again but this is an exception to the rule and it becomes very obvious from the context. *The rule is that the present tense of a verb denotes duration, i.e. denotes that something "goes on" happening.* Applying this rule, John 3:14-18 would read[9]:

John 3:14-18
"And as Moses lifted up the serpent in the wilderness, so must the Son of Man be lifted up, that *whoever goes on believing in him may have eternal life.* "For God so loved the world, that he gave his only Son, *that whoever goes on believing in him should not perish but have eternal life.* For God did not send his Son into the world to condemn the world, but in order that the world might be saved through him. *Whoever goes on believing in him is not condemned,* but whoever does not believe is condemned already, because he has not believed in the name of the only Son of God."

The promises of John 3:14-18 are in no way promises to people who once upon a time believed but eventually moved

---

[9] For more on this see David Pawson: "Is John 3:16 the gospel?", pp. 38-45, TerraNova Publications, 2007.

away without returning. In contrast, they are to people who believe now, in the present, and they go on believing.

Understanding that the present tense in Greek indicates duration, i.e. that something goes on happening can really revolutionalise the way we understand many passages. My suggestion would be that whenever you see the present tense ("believes", "forgives" etc.) replace it, after checking the context, with the construction "goes on" + the present participle ( for example: "goes on believing", "goes on forgiving" etc.). This will perhaps change the way you read many passages.

# APPENDIX 2

## ARE THE TEACHINGS OF THE GOSPELS, INCLUDING THE "HARD SAYINGS", FOR US?

Many will consider this question as rather unnecessary and say that, of course, the gospels are relevant to us. But there are some who implicitly or explicitly believe, that the gospels do not have such importance for they do not, according to their view, refer to us but to Jews, living under the age of law. Foundation of this theory is the so called dispensationalism, which taken into the extreme concludes that relevant to the believers of today are only the epistles (and in some extreme forms of dispensationalism, only parts of them!), while the remaining Word of God is rather for our information only. Indeed, the Bible contains parts that are not for the application of the Christian. For example, the law with its ordinances, is something that covers a big part of Exodus, Leviticus, Deuteronomy and Numbers. As the law of Moses is no longer valid (Hebrews 8:13, Colossians 2:13-14) we would be right to say that these parts are not there for our direct application but rather for our information and benefit. This does not, of course, happen for everything in the Old Testament. Psalms and Proverbs, for example, are books of eternal truths that have no connection to a particular age. The same is also true for many prophetic writings.

So, instead of what many do, classifying the part before the gospels as "Old Testament" (those who support that the gospels are not relevant to us, put this separation in Acts), I would rather pay attention and read what is said and then ask myself whether there is a reason that what I read could possibly not refer to me. To say it differently instead of breaking the Word of God into parts like Old Testament and New Testament (which are human divisions anyway) I would rather take the Word of God, as ONE and evaluate whether there are reasons that something would perhaps not refer to me. Thus, much in Numbers or Deuteronomy etc. does not refer to me: it relates to the Old Covenant and those living under it. I have reasons to not apply the killing of goats, the various sacrifices etc. as these are obsolete: Jesus Christ gave His blood once and for all and no other sacrifice is needed. The same we could say about the law of the Sabbath, the law of the tithe etc. I can learn from them but they are no longer a law valid for my direct application.

Moving to Jesus now and His teachings, some have taken the fact that when Jesus was speaking the law was still there, being fulfilled by Him (it was fully fulfilled with His crucifixion), and based on this they support that what Jesus said does not refer to us but to people under the law. Thus parts of the epistles are elevated and the gospels are downgraded as not that relevant to us, hence creating an artificial antithesis between Jesus and the writings of His very disciples. I believe this is wrong, for though Jesus lived in an age when the law was valid and was still being fulfilled by Him, *He did not come to teach about the Mosaic law!* What was His mission then? Why was He sent? Let's allow Him to give the answer. This He does in Luke 4:43 where we read:

"But he said to them, "I must preach *the good news of the kingdom of God* to the other towns as well; *for I was sent for this purpose.*"

The purpose for which Jesus was sent was to preach the good news of *the Kingdom of God*. He did not come to preach just some good news, but something specific: the good news of the

Kingdom of God, the good news that the Kingdom of God is coming! The preaching about the coming Kingdom of God, was – as He Himself said - the very reason He was sent!

Matthew 4:17 verifies very clearly that the Kingdom of God (or Kingdom of heaven, as it is called in Matthew) was the start and remained the main subject of Jesus' teaching:

Matthew 4:17
"From that time Jesus began to preach, saying, "Repent, for *the kingdom of heaven* is at hand."

And again after a few verses:

Matthew 4:23
"And he went throughout all Galilee, teaching in their synagogues and *proclaiming the gospel of the kingdom* and healing every disease and every affliction among the people."

What was Jesus preaching was not the law but the gospel of the Kingdom of God. Then in his first recorded in Matthew teaching, the so called sermon of the mount, we find Him opening it as follows:

Matthew 5:2-3
"And he opened his mouth and taught them, saying: "Blessed are the poor in spirit, for theirs is the *kingdom of heaven*."

Furthermore in Luke 8:1
"Soon afterward he went on through cities and villages, *proclaiming and bringing the good news of the kingdom of God*".

And Luke 9:59-60
"To another he said, "Follow me." But he said, "Lord, let me first go and bury my father." And Jesus said to him, "Leave the dead to bury their own dead. But as for you, *go and proclaim the kingdom of God*."

The phrases "kingdom of God" and its synonym "kingdom of heaven" occur in total 84 times in the gospels. The Kingdom of God was the main subject of the teaching of the Master. So guess what: *what He mainly spoke about and which is recorded in the gospels is about the kingdom of God – Jesus' main subject and mission - and not about the law,* though of course since the law had not yet been fulfilled but was being fulfilled, you can see things here and there referring to the law. But in no way can somebody classify the message of Jesus as referring only to the Jews living under the law. In contrast, the message of Jesus was about the good news of the Kingdom of God and how to enter into it. Is not this, the entering into the Kingdom of God, the main goal for me and you? If yes, let us pay attention to what *the* specialist on the matter, the King Himself says about it, instead of making the grave error of essentially putting Him aside as not relevant to us.

Moving on, let us look at what Jesus was speaking about with His disciples after He was raised from the dead and until His ascension. In Acts 1:3 we find a summary of it:

"He presented himself alive to them after his suffering by many proofs, *appearing to them during forty days and speaking about the kingdom of God.*"

The Kingdom of God was not something that Jesus was teaching only before His crucifixion or just a topic among many others. In contrast it was chief topic, *the* chief topic I would say, of His ministry. He was preaching about it before the crucifixion and continued to speak about it after the resurrection too, all the way up to the time of his ascension. Now what did the disciples do after the ascension? Was there a change of policy? Again the book of Acts gives us the answer:

Philip, preached the Kingdom of God (Acts 8:12):

"But when they believed Philip as *he preached good news about the kingdom of God* and the name of Jesus Christ, they were baptized, both men and women."

Paul and Barnabas, preached about the Kingdom of God and how to enter it, which apparently is "through many tribulations":

Acts 14: 21-22
"When they had preached the gospel to that city and had made many disciples, they returned to Lystra and to Iconium and to Antioch, strengthening the souls of the disciples, *encouraging them to continue in the faith,* and *saying that through many tribulations we must enter the kingdom of God."*

Paul again, this time in Ephesus:
Acts 19:8
"And he entered the synagogue and for three months spoke boldly, reasoning *and persuading them about the kingdom of God."*

Paul, now in Rome, in arrest:
Acts 28:23
"When they had appointed a day for him, they came to him at his lodging in greater numbers. From morning till evening he expounded to them, *testifying to the kingdom of God* and trying to convince them about Jesus both from the Law of Moses and from the Prophets."

And the book of Acts closes as follows, referring to this great apostle:

Acts 28:30-31
"He lived there two whole years at his own expense, and welcomed all who came to him, *proclaiming the kingdom of God* and teaching about the Lord Jesus Christ with all boldness and without hindrance."

To summarize: the Kingdom of God was the purpose that Jesus was sent. He preached about it all the time, all the way up to His ascension. Then the apostles took over and did the same. Paul preached about the Kingdom of God proclaiming it all the way till the end of his life. The same did Philip and I am sure all the others too. We see therefore that the message did not vary: both Jesus and His apostles were preaching about the Kingdom of God. It is a grave error to downgrade the gospels as supposedly being part of the law, because though the law was still being fulfilled, what the gospels mainly describe, what their main theme is, is the Kingdom of God and not the law.

The gospels therefore have *much* more to do with the new era we are living in than with the old era of the law. This is especially so for the parts we read previously in chapter 3 of this study, which were in fact addressed to His disciples and were given – most of them - just hours before His arrest. To the question then: are these passages for us, the answer is short and simple: yes, they are. If we are disciples of Christ, people who want to enter into the Kingdom of God, what both the Master and His apostles say is relevant to us and they do not contradict each other. How could they, anyway? Here is what the Lord commanded His disciples just before His ascension:

Matthew 28:18-20
"And Jesus came and said to them, "All authority in heaven and on earth has been given to me. Go therefore and make disciples of all nations, baptizing them in the name of the Father and of the Son and of the Holy Spirit, *teaching them to observe all that I have commanded you.* And behold, I am with you always, to the end of the age."

The Lord commanded the apostles to make disciples and teach them to observe "all that I have commanded you". "I have commanded you" is in the past tense. Therefore it was not new revelation He was speaking about here, but commandments and teachings that He had *already* given to them and there is only one place where these already given teachings and commandments of the Lord are recorded: the gospels.

So, are the gospels, the sayings of Christ, and in particular His sayings to His disciples, relevant to the Christian of today? Absolutely! Let us make no mistake about it.

# APPENDIX 3

## REVELATION 2, 3: ARE THE EPISTLES OF JESUS TO THE SEVEN CHURCHES RELEVANT TO US?

After the gospels and with the exception of some very small passages in Acts and the epistles, it is in Revelation where we find Jesus speaking again in the first person. Chapters 2 and 3 contain letters that were sent to seven churches in Minor Asia. Jesus directly dictated these letters to the apostle John, commanding him to write them down, and send them to these churches, together with the whole book. It is surprising however how little attention these epistles of Jesus receive. Similar to the theory that essentially puts aside the gospels by classifying them as not relevant to us, one theory put forward is that these epistles of Jesus, together with the book of Revelation as a whole, do not really refer to us. Instead they refer – according to this theory - to some future believers and they are going to understand the book of Revelation, implicitly meaning that we can safely ignore this book or consider it as something "just for our information". Concerning the seven churches, these are, so the theory goes, future churches and to them these letters refer[10]. However, *these*

---

[10] Of course there are many other theories concerning the meaning of the book of Revelation, almost all of which are missing the relevancy of the epistles to the seven churches (this is the focus of this appendix) and they treat them not as real

*churches were real churches when John wrote the letters, exactly as there was a real church in Corinth to which Paul addressed his letter.* In fact, some of these churches, such as the church of Ephesus and Laodicea, we can find in Paul's letters as well. Truly, the whole argument of these epistles not really referring to believers living under the age of grace breaks down if we see what Jesus Himself ordered John to do with the message he was about to receive. This is given in no unclear terms in Revelation 1:11

Revelation 1:11
"Write what you see in a book *and send it to the seven churches*, to Ephesus and to Smyrna and to Pergamum and to Thyatira and to Sardis and to Philadelphia and to Laodicea."

So guess what John did? He wrote it and sent it right away to the seven churches mentioned. Therefore, the letters of Jesus to these churches refer to Christian believers in these churches and they are as much relevant to us, as the letters of Paul sent for example to believers in the church of Corinth, Ephesus, Galatia etc.

One of the reasons why some people haste to put these letters in the pretty big box they have with the name "not relevant to us" is because they essentially do not like what Jesus says. They see Jesus saying for example: "I know your works" (Revelation 2:2), "repent and do the works you did at first. If not, I will come to you and remove your lampstand from its place, unless you repent" (Revelation 2:5) etc. and they realize that such and similar – "harsh" according to them – sayings do not reconcile with what they believe as the gospel and their image of Jesus. Therefore, ways have to be devised to avoid it as much as possible. And the way which many find is to consider these letters and Revelation in general as mainly referring to future believers that will be living in those days. The truth however is that they are as relevant to us as the epistles of the apostles: both kinds of epistles were written for

---

epistles addressed to real people in real churches but as something either metaphoric or past, with not present application, or future with also no present application.

real churches and real believers of that time and therefore both refer by extension also to us.

Going now to the epistles themselves, we see there that the way Jesus is looking at each church (and the church is not a building but people) is like a coach who cares about his athletes who are running a race or fighting a fight. So you will see that the feedback to these churches is different in each case. A couple of them are faring well. They should keep up like this. But the rest of them are having problems. The Lord does not tell them "you know it is OK.. I have paid the price so that you do not have to do anything." Instead what He does is after telling them their good points (this He did to all except to the church of Laodicea) He passes on to the criticism He has for them. In four out of the seven churches He tells them "Repent", change course! In fact He does not tell them just "Repent" but "Repent *or else..*". Here are some:

Revelation 2:5
"Remember therefore from where you have fallen; *repent* and do the first works, *or else* I will come to you quickly and remove your lampstand from its place–unless you repent."

Revelation 2:15-16
"Thus you also have those who hold the doctrine of the Nicolaitans, which thing I hate. *Repent, or else* I will come to you quickly and will fight against them with the sword of My mouth."

Revelation 3:2-3
"Be watchful …. hold fast and *repent*. Therefore if you will not watch, I will come upon you as a thief, and you will not know what hour I will come upon you."

Some cannot comprehend that their Jesus would have ever spoken like this to churches. But dear brothers the Bible shows us Jesus from various angles and one of them is in Revelation 1:11-18:

Revelation 1:11-18

"Write what you see in a book and send it to the seven churches, to Ephesus and to Smyrna and to Pergamum and to Thyatira and to Sardis and to Philadelphia and to Laodicea." Then I turned to see the voice that was speaking to me, and on turning I saw seven golden lampstands, and in the midst of the lampstands one like a son of man, clothed with a long robe and with a golden sash around his chest. The hairs of his head were white, like white wool, like snow. His eyes were like a flame of fire, his feet were like burnished bronze, refined in a furnace, and his voice was like the roar of many waters. In his right hand he held seven stars, from his mouth came a sharp two-edged sword, and his face was like the sun shining in full strength. When I saw him, I fell at his feet as though dead. But he laid his right hand on me, saying, "Fear not, I am the first and the last, and the living one. I died, and behold I am alive forevermore, and I have the keys of Death and Hades."

Does our view or image of Jesus has space for the above picture also or is Jesus for us just a sweet little blond young man with blue eyes that would not touch a fly?

To go back to our original question: do the epistles of Jesus to the seven churches refer to us too by extension, exactly as the epistles of Paul to the Galatians or the Corinthians refer also to us by extension? The answer is yes they do. All were supposed to be read and be acted upon by their respective listeners. And if we have an ear –as we should – for the epistles of the apostles to the churches, so also we should have an ear for the epistles of the apostles' Master to the churches.

"He who has an ear, let him hear what the Spirit says to the churches." (Revelation 2 and 3).

## ABOUT THE AUTHOR

I am a Greek Christian born in 1969 and living since many years in Germany. I am married with three children. I am teaching the Word of God since 1994 and I have been the main author and publisher of the Journal of Biblical Accuracy, a Bible teaching magazine and perhaps one of the first to appear online (in 1996). The related address is: http://www.jba.gr and there are hundreds of articles in many different languages. Please visit the site and subscribe for free to receive more.

This is the second book I have written. The first one is titled "Tithing, giving and the New Testament" and as this one is available for free to read and download on my website.

On the private side: I earn my living by working as a business consultant. I am traveling every day about 100 Km by train to reach my work place. It is true to say that most of the work for this book has been done in trains commuting to work. I am not affiliated to any organization nor am I supported financially by one. I am by education an Economist, having also a Ph.D. on the subject. I am speaking Greek (mother tongue), English and German. My aspirations? To run the race of faith to end and to be a fruitful disciple of my Lord, loving Him and my neighbor as myself and living the Word in practice.

Made in the USA
San Bernardino, CA
19 July 2015